Contents

Abbreviations

CIO	Chief Information Officer
DME	development, modernization, and enhancement
IT	information technology
OMB	Office of Management and Budget
SSA	Social Security Administration

United States Government Accountability Office
Washington, DC 20548

April 26, 2012

The Honorable Sam Johnson
Chairman
Subcommittee on Social Security
Committee on Ways and Means
House of Representatives

Dear Mr. Chairman:

The Social Security Administration (SSA) is responsible for delivering Social Security services that touch the lives of virtually every American. To provide these services, the agency manages and funds a variety of information technology (IT) initiatives ranging from those supporting the processing and payment of Disability Insurance and Supplemental Security Income benefits to those that facilitate the calculation and withholding of Medicare premiums. Last fiscal year, the agency spent nearly $1.6 billion for IT.

Because of challenges SSA faces with its aging IT systems, the agency has committed to investing in the capacity and modern technologies needed to update its aging and strained IT infrastructure,[1] and has initiated efforts toward modernization. In addition, it has recently undertaken a major realignment of its IT governance structure, including realigning the responsibilities of the Chief Information Officer (CIO).

Given the importance of IT in supporting SSA's ability to meet its mission, you requested that we examine the agency's modernization efforts. As agreed with your office, our specific objectives were to (1) determine SSA's progress in modernizing its IT systems and capabilities; (2) evaluate the effectiveness of SSA's plans and strategy for modernizing its systems and capabilities; and (3) assess whether the realignment of the agency's CIO responsibilities allows for effective oversight and management of the systems modernization efforts.

---

[1]IT infrastructure refers to the computer hardware, computer software, telecommunications, data, and technology-governance components that underlie the agency's entire enterprise.

To determine SSA's modernization progress, we evaluated project descriptions along with their supporting documentation to determine modernization improvements and enhancements and compared them with activities described in Office of Management and Budget (OMB) exhibit 53 and 300 guidance.[2] We reviewed agency IT project plans, milestones, goals, performance metrics, budgets, briefings, IT investment review board minutes, and project oversight documentation. We also interviewed relevant program officials in the agency's major IT areas to identify and obtain descriptions of SSA's key modernization initiatives from 2001 to 2011. In addition, we reviewed the agency's established performance measures for 17 major IT projects for 2010 and 2011 and compared them to federal law and guidance.[3]

To evaluate the effectiveness of SSA's plans and strategy for modernizing its systems and capabilities, we analyzed the agency's IT systems modernization plans against guidance in OMB's *Circular A-130*, on managing federal information resources. Additionally, we assessed the agency's enterprise architecture documentation against OMB's *Federal Enterprise Architecture* guidance and our enterprise architecture framework[4] to determine the effectiveness of its enterprise architecture in describing and supporting its modernization efforts.

To determine whether SSA's CIO realignment allows for effective oversight and management, we reviewed SSA's plans for and analyses of the reassignment of CIO duties and functions. We also reviewed documentation, such as updated agency policy, memos, and IT investment review board minutes, and interviewed the CIO and other IT executives about their roles and responsibilities under the new IT realignment.

---

[2]Each year, agencies submit to OMB a Capital Asset Plan and Business Case—the exhibit 300—to justify each request for a major IT investment. In addition, each federal agency reports its IT investment portfolio annually to OMB via an exhibit 53. The exhibit 53 provides budget estimates for IT investments and identifies those that are major investments and nonmajor investments. OMB uses the exhibit 53 to create an overall "Federal IT Investment Portfolio" published as part of the President's Budget.

[3]The Government Performance and Results Act, Clinger-Cohen Act, and OMB's *Federal Enterprise Architecture*.

[4]GAO, *Organizational Transformation: A Framework for Assessing and Improving Enterprise Architecture Management (Version 2.0)*, GAO-10-846G (Washington, D.C.: August 2010).

To assess the reliability of the data that we used to support the findings in this report, we reviewed relevant program documentation to substantiate evidence obtained through interviews with agency officials. We determined that the data used in this report are sufficiently reliable.

We conducted this performance audit from May 2011 to April 2012 in accordance with generally accepted government auditing standards. Those standards require that we plan and perform the audit to obtain sufficient, appropriate evidence to provide a reasonable basis for our findings and conclusions based on our audit objectives. We believe that the evidence obtained provides a reasonable basis for our findings and conclusions based on our audit objectives. Additional details on our objectives, scope, and methodology are provided in appendix I.

Background

SSA's mission is to deliver Social Security services that meet the changing needs of the public. The Social Security Act and amendments[5] established the programs that SSA administers. The Old Age, Survivors, and Disability Insurance program—commonly referred to as Social Security—is one of the nation's largest entitlement programs. Financed by two trust funds, this program provides monthly benefits to retired and disabled workers, their spouses, children, and the survivors of insured workers.[6] According to SSA, in fiscal year 2011, about 54 million people received benefits from this program as a retiree, spouse, disabled person, or other dependent. In addition, Supplemental Security Income is a needs-based program that is financed from general tax revenues. It is designed to provide benefits to aged adults and to blind or disabled adults and children who have limited income and resources. According to SSA, in 2011, over 8 million people received Supplemental Security Income benefits.[7] Collectively, about 155 million people work and pay Social Security taxes. The agency's fiscal year 2011 expenses totaled about $12.4 billion to support programs administered by SSA.

[5]42 U.S.C. Chapter 7.

[6]This program was established by Title II of the Social Security Act and is sometimes referred to as "Title II."

[7]The Supplemental Security Income program was established by Title XVI of the Social Security Act and is sometimes referred to as "Title XVI."

Organizationally, SSA is very large. It is headed by the Commissioner, who is assisted by the Deputy Commissioner and various other executive officials, including the Chief and Deputy Chief of Staff, Executive Secretary, and nine deputy commissioners who are responsible for the agency's various business components. Figure 1 provides a simplified SSA organization chart.

Figure 1: Organization of the Social Security Administration

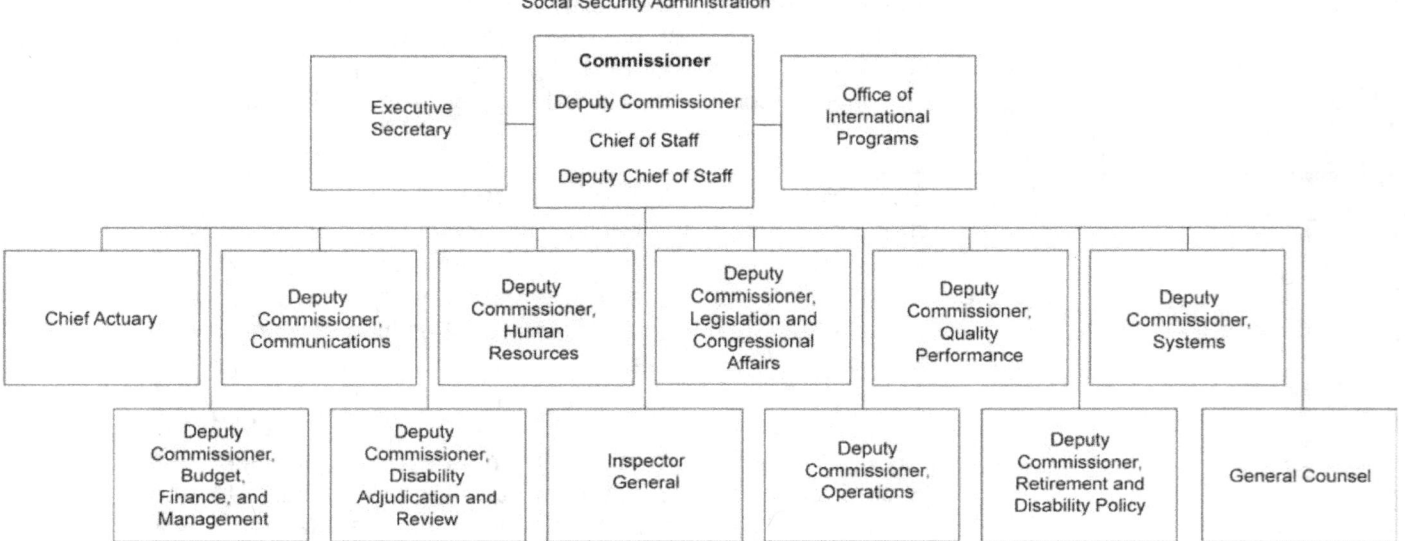

Source: SSA data.

The Commissioner is supported by about 65,000 federal and 15,000 state employees who are located at headquarters and throughout a decentralized network of more than 1,500 offices that includes regional offices, field offices, teleservice centers, processing centers, program service centers, hearing offices, and state Disability Determination Services. In support of its operations, the component offices perform an assortment of interrelated and interdependent business functions, including financial, operational, legislative, policy, and performance management.

SSA has defined five core business processes to facilitate planning and managing the delivery of services to beneficiaries: (1) issuing Social Security numbers (enumeration process); (2) establishing and maintaining individual records of earnings; (3) processing benefits claims;

(4) maintaining post-entitlement records of changes and reviews; and (5) informing the public. These core business processes cross program and organizational lines within the agency. Although the focus of each of these processes is to serve members of the public, each also entails important interaction with other entities. For example, while the issuance of Social Security numbers is a service to individual members of the public, the verification of them is an important service to business and other governmental agencies, such as state and federal partners processing individuals' applications for welfare benefits and local departments of motor vehicles issuing a driver's license.

IT Environment and Challenges

SSA relies extensively on IT hardware and software to carry out its core mission functions. Specifically, IT systems are used to administer its programs and support related administrative needs that include, among other things,

- handling millions of transactions on SSA's toll-free telephone number;

- maintaining records for the millions of beneficiaries and recipients of SSA's programs, including Supplemental Security Income, Retirement, and Disability Insurance;

- evaluating evidence and making determinations of eligibility for benefits on new claims;

- issuing new and replacement Social Security cards;

- processing earnings items for crediting to workers' earnings records;

- processing continuing disability reviews;[8] and

- processing non-disability Supplemental Security Income redeterminations.[9]

---

[8]For beneficiaries found eligible for disability benefits, SSA periodically conducts medical disability reviews to determine whether beneficiaries are still medically eligible for benefits. SSA also conducts reviews of beneficiaries' earnings and work activity, as appropriate, to determine if they are still financially eligible to receive disability benefits. SSA refers to these non-medical reviews as "work CDRs."

The agency's technology infrastructure is housed at its National Computer Center in Maryland and its Second Support Center in North Carolina, which are co-processing data centers for all enterprise operations. The agency also has network service delivery points in Missouri and California. These centers collectively house servers and databases that store petabytes[10] of SSA data containing Social Security numbers, employment history and wage earnings, and lifelong history of relevant information on individual status, such as marital status and address. The data housed in SSA's computer centers are accessed through a variety of databases, including its Master Data Access Method database system,[11] which was developed in house by SSA in the 1980s originally to convert from tape to disk storage of data, as well as other vendor-supported database systems.[12]

To carry out day-to-day processes, SSA uses mainframes, desktop computers, and servers, which generally run Windows operating systems, and SSA personnel use enterprise Web and client-server applications. These include administrative, management information, and programmatic software applications.

In fiscal year 2011, SSA reported that its IT infrastructure supported the payment of more than $770 billion in benefits to approximately 60 million people, and the maintenance of hundreds of millions of Social Security numbers and related earnings records for nearly every American. The agency expects to rely more and more on electronic functionality to process its growing workloads in the future.

---

[9]SSA conducts periodic reviews to determine if SSI beneficiaries are still eligible to receive SSI payments based on the beneficiary's income, living arrangement, and other non-medical factors related to SSI—these reviews are referred to as SSI redeterminations.

[10]A petabyte is a unit of information equal to one quadrillion bytes, or 1,000 terabytes.

[11]The Master Data Access Method database is used to support the storage and retrieval of SSA's major program master files. The database was developed in the early 1980s and was written using a programming language that is no longer widely used. SSA is in the process of converting its mission support data from its Master Data Access Method file management system to a more modern Database Management System, Database 2, (DB2), which is a relational database product and includes a range of application development and management tools.

[12]SSA uses a variety of databases, including Database 2 and Structured Query Language (SQL).

Many of SSA's existing systems were developed in the 1960s and 1970s, and while the agency has performed technical and functional upgrades throughout the years to accommodate legislative and policy changes, these legacy systems have aged. Accordingly, as they have aged, these systems have presented various challenges to the efficiency of SSA's existing IT environment. Specifically:

- Many of its programs are written in COBOL, which is one of the oldest computer programming languages and is difficult to maintain.[13]

- SSA is required to store, process, and share increasing amounts of data with public- and private-sector partners.

- There is an increasing need to transition to Web-based online access for SSA data and services.

- Many of the National Computer Center's building infrastructure systems are well past their designed life cycle. SSA has expressed concerns that the center could deteriorate to the point that a major failure to the building systems could jeopardize its ability to handle increasing workloads without interruption. As a result, SSA is developing a new data center to replace the existing Baltimore, Maryland, center.

- While SSA has begun conversion to a more efficient database system for its critical mission support files and uses more modern databases for its new applications, the agency continues to use its Master Data Access Method database system, which does not support industry standards for automatic data access. Conversion to a more modern database has not been completed for one of its largest files—the Master Beneficiary Record file.

---

[13]COBOL (Common Business Oriented Language) is a business application programming language that was introduced in the 1960s. This language is generally viewed as obsolete, making it difficult to implement new business processes and new service delivery models, such as online, real-time processing. SSA has roughly 60 million lines of COBOL in production that support the agency's high transaction volume and enable the agency to meet its regulatory, benefit, and reporting requirements. According to SSA, new applications are being developed in a more modern programming language, for example Java, and as a result the percentage of programs using COBOL is declining.

In its enterprisewide Agency Strategic Plan covering fiscal years 2013 through 2016, SSA identified IT as one of the key foundational elements to achieving success in meeting all four of its agencywide goals.[14]

Recognizing the challenges to its IT environment, SSA has stated that it plans to:

- develop and implement a common disability case processing system for all 54 state Disability Determination Services and obtain electronic authorizations for supporting records that is intended to help reduce processing times and disability backlogs;

- increase the use of online services to enable individuals to file for benefits and access and update personal information;

- develop new tools and automated means for beneficiaries to report changes, such as changes to their disabling condition's status, to help increase efforts to accurately pay benefits;

- continue its efforts to modernize systems to help ensure information is reported electronically, to reduce error-prone and expensive manual processes; and

- increase public satisfaction with new telephone services by replacing its national 800-number telecommunications infrastructure with a new state-of-the-art system that is expected to eliminate lengthy navigation menus that frustrate the public and provide additional lines for callers.

SSA's enterprisewide Agency Strategic Plan outlines goals to achieve a modern data center building while maintaining system performance. Specifically, IT modernization is to be achieved by transitioning to the agency's new data center; using advanced cyber-security tools to protect its data and systems; using proven new technologies to improve IT cost, performance, and data-loss risk; and incrementally modernizing its older software applications based on business opportunity and technical risk.

---

[14]SSA's 2013 to 2016 Agency Strategic Plan lists four key strategic goals: Deliver Quality Disability Decisions and Services, Provide Quality Service to the Public, Preserve the Public's Trust in Our Programs, and Strengthen Our Workforce and Infrastructure.

GAO-12-495 Information Technology

SSA Spends Significant Resources on IT

Over the last 12 years, SSA's annual funding for IT has generally increased, with some decline over the last 2 fiscal years. Specifically, it spent about $691 million in fiscal year 2001 and about $1.6 billion in fiscal year 2011. The agency is estimating that it will spend about $1.4 billion on IT in fiscal year 2012.

Figure 2: SSA IT Funding for Fiscal Years 2001 through 2012

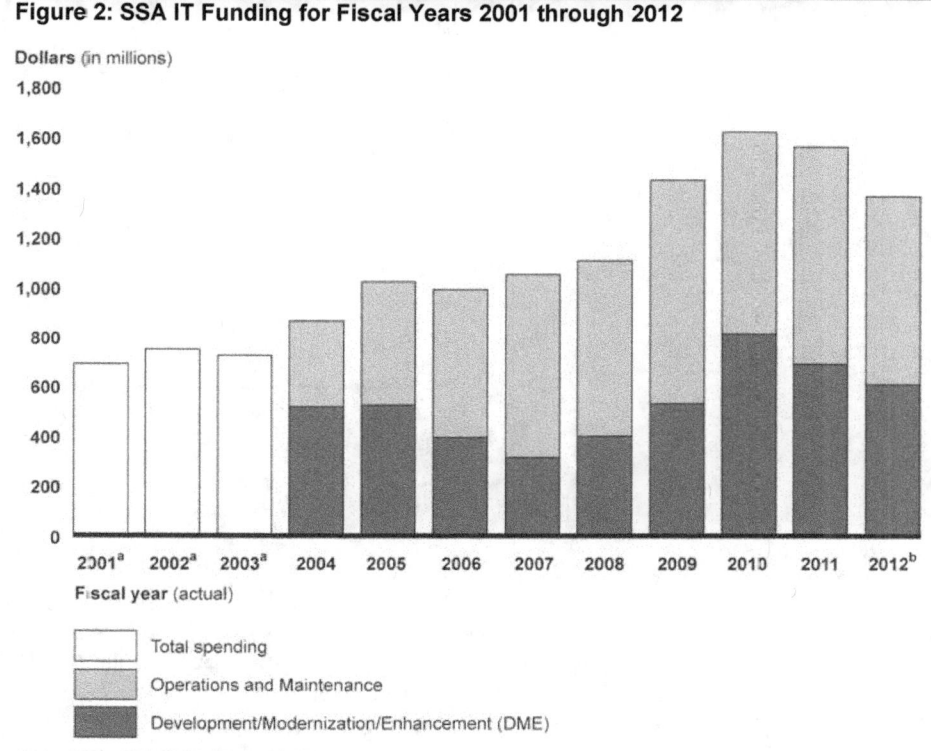

Source: GAO analysis of SSA exhibit 53 data.

[a]According to SSA, for fiscal year 2001, OMB did not require funding to be identified by DME or Operations and Maintenance, and for fiscal years 2002 and 2003, DME and Operations and Maintenance expenditures were only required by OMB for major projects. SSA further noted that for fiscal years 2002 and 2003, DME funding was $244.8 and $341.7 million respectively, and Operations and Maintenance funding was $94.2 and $160.9 million, respectively.

[b]The fiscal year 2012 numbers are appropriated funds as of February 2012.

As reflected in figure 2, the agency's budget for IT investments includes money for maintenance of existing system operations (referred to as "operations and maintenance") and for enhancements to existing systems and modernization of legacy application systems (collectively referred to as "development, modernization, and enhancement" or "DME").

Figure 3: SSA IT Spending for Development, Modernization, and Enhancement and Operations and Maintenance from 2004 to 2011

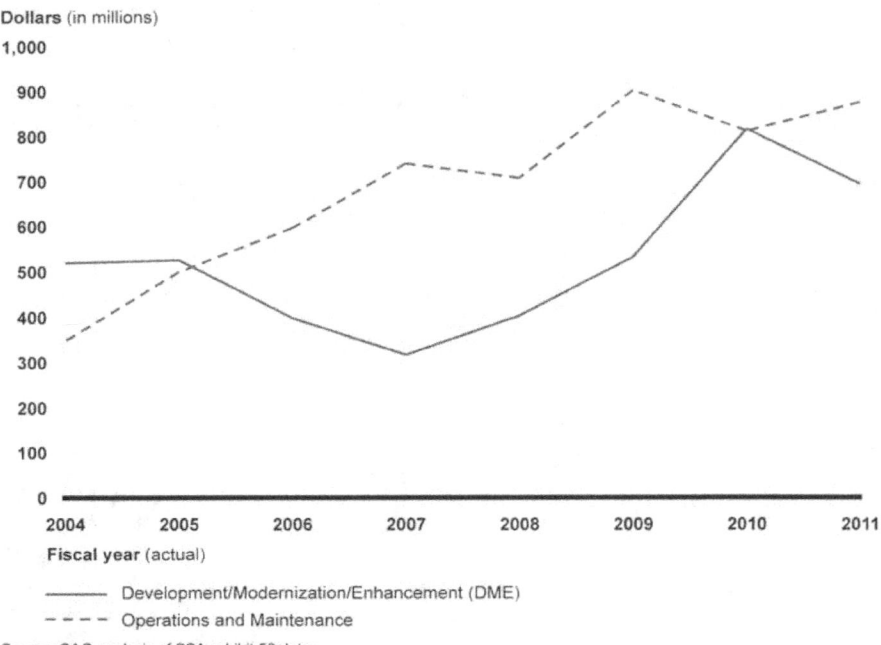

Source: GAO analysis of SSA exhibit 53 data.

As shown in figure 3, during the period from 2004 to 2011, the agency's development, modernization, and enhancement expenditures increased from $520 million to $693 million. Further, the agency's expenditures for operations and maintenance have also increased, from $348 million in 2004 to $875 million in 2011.

SSA's annual spending supports the agency's data center, mainframe, client-server desktops, a commercial off-the-shelf financial accounting system, and many projects to maintain and modernize IT systems. Each year, the agency works on hundreds of individual IT projects that vary in size and scope; some adapt existing program operations to accommodate legislative changes or to enhance existing processes, while others upgrade aging technology to ensure continued vendor support.

IT Governance Structure

SSA's Office of Systems is responsible for developing, overseeing, and maintaining the agency's IT systems. With approximately 3,300 IT staff, the Office of Systems comprises eight component offices:

- Office of Telecommunications and System Operations—responsible for the computer systems and networks.

- Office of Systems Electronic Services—directs the development of software that supports electronic service-delivery initiatives.

- Office of Applications and Supplemental Security Income Systems—responsible for most phases in the systems development life cycle for the Supplemental Security Income, Quality Assurance, Customer Help Information, and Representative Payee programs.

- Office of Retirement and Survivors Insurance Systems—responsible for programmatic and management information systems for these systems as well as for the Disability Insurance program.

- Office of Earnings, Enumeration and Administrative Systems—designs, develops, and maintains SSA's earnings, enumeration, and administrative systems.

- Office of Disability Systems—develops, implements, and maintains electronic systems to support disability programs.

- Office of Enterprise Support, Architecture, and Engineering—identifies the strategic IT resources needed to support SSA business processes and operations.

- Office of Information Security—manages and directs SSA's overall information systems security program.

The agency's IT governance structure for review and management of its IT investments, documented in its Capital Planning and Investment Control guidance,[15] assigns responsibility for the investment management process to SSA executive-level managers. Specifically, the Strategic

---

[15]SSA officials reported that they are in the process of updating the Capital Planning and Investment Control guide to, among other things, address lessons learned from an assessment of the Strategic Information Technology Assessment and Review board process.

Information Technology Assessment and Review board is responsible for establishing priorities and making recommendations for the agency's 2-year IT plan, which specifies which projects and systems the agency will build and operate. The board, which meets quarterly, is comprised of the Principal Deputy Commissioner, the other deputy commissioners, and other senior executives and is chaired by the Deputy Commissioner for Systems (who also is SSA's CIO). This official provides advice to the Commissioner and makes final IT budget recommendations.

SSA's IT investments are divided among portfolios. These portfolios are aligned with the goals and objectives described in the enterprisewide Agency Strategic Plan. For fiscal year 2011, SSA maintained nine portfolios for the following areas: core services, cross-cutting, disability process, hearings process, high-performing workforce, program integrity, savings and solvency, SSA infrastructure, and Social Security number process. Portfolios are assigned to deputy commissioners and their teams, to assist in the day-to-day management of the corresponding investment portfolio within each business component.

Table 1 lists key IT management responsibilities of participants in SSA's Capital Planning and Investment Control process.

Table 1: Roles and Responsibilities in the Select Phase of SSA's Capital Planning and Investment Control Process

Key participants	Membership/description	Key responsibilities
Deputy Commissioner for Systems/CIO	Heads the Office of Systems	Ensures that IT is acquired in accordance with the Capital Planning and Investment Control procedures
		Chairs the Strategic Information Technology Assessment and Review board
		Reviews and obtains Commissioner approval of the annual IT budget and the agency IT plan
		Oversees systems development and operations
Deputy commissioners and other top-level executives	Heads of organizational units responsible for business areas and corresponding portfolios	Achieves portfolio objectives that correspond to the agency's strategic goals
		Provides recommendations for the annual IT plan
Strategic Information Technology Assessment and Review board	Deputy Commissioner for Systems/CIO is the chairman and members are the Principal Deputy Commissioner, deputy commissioners, and other senior executives responsible for the business units	Provides guidance on agency priorities
		Reviews and makes recommendations on the agency IT plan
		Oversees performance of IT projects

Key participants	Membership/description	Key responsibilities
Office of Systems Planning Staff	IT support staff	Provides the Strategic Information Technology Assessment and Review board with updated status on the agency's major investments
		Publishes agency IT planning material
		Provides agency support for all Strategic Information Technology Assessment and Review board-related activities
		Documents policies and procedures in support of the capital planning and investment control process
		Provides guidance and support to business sponsor components for all planning activities on IT proposal submissions
Sponsor	Owner of an IT proposal	Represents the component and provides strategic direction
		Describes the proposed project and business or user needs
		Works with the Office of Systems to establish project requirements and level of effort estimates
Portfolio team	Stakeholders representing projects in a portfolio	Reviews sponsor proposals and recommends items for review in support of the agency strategic objectives
		Prepares a recommendation for specific IT proposals for the agency IT plan
Portfolio team support staff	Staff responsible for supporting the portfolio executive and portfolio team	Manages all portfolio-related activities
		Prepares portfolio team deliverables
		Serves as the liaison between the business sponsor and the Office of Systems
Portfolio Executive	Senior-level manager	Ensures that the portfolio team and stakeholders follow agencywide guidance
		Ensures the objectives of the portfolio are aligned with the Agency Strategic Plan
		Works with portfolio stakeholders to develop proposal recommendations that reflect an enterprise perspective
		Monitors and reports the performance of the portfolio to the Strategic Information Technology Assessment and Review board

Source: GAO analysis of SSA data.

SSA uses its established Capital Planning and Investment Control process to manage its software development projects. The investment management process is intended to meet the objectives of the Clinger-

Cohen Act[16] by providing a framework for selecting, controlling, and evaluating investments to help ensure they meet the strategic and business objectives of the agency.

During the *investment selection* phase, new projects are to be proposed by a sponsor—either from a business unit for mission-related projects or from the Office of Systems—and assigned to one of the nine portfolios. Proposals that identify business needs are to be developed based on the Commissioner's priorities or gap analyses performed by each portfolio team. The portfolio executives and their teams are to review business-sponsored IT investment proposals and recommend and submit proposals to the Office of Systems to develop resource estimates on the proposals. In response, each portfolio executive is to develop a prioritized list of proposed projects using several factors, such as the availability of agency resources, and prepare a recommendation of specific proposals for the agency IT plan. Next, the prioritized lists are to be combined into a proposed agency IT plan for approval by the Strategic Information Technology Assessment and Review board. The plan is to be comprised of proposed investments for the next 2 fiscal years, and provide information on work-year requirements. In addition, expected benefits and returns on investment are to be included for new development projects. The Strategic Information Technology Assessment and Review board is responsible for approving the agency IT plan on an annual basis and is to modify the plan as needed by changing priorities. According to the Deputy Commissioner for Systems, the Commissioner is to then provide final approval of the specific proposals for the agency IT plan.

During the *control* phase, the Office of Systems is responsible for holding monthly meetings with IT project managers who are assigned to monitor projects that are in development. During these meetings, projects that are not meeting cost and schedule expectations are to be identified and corrective actions initiated. According to SSA guidance, one of the objectives of the meetings is to resolve problems related to underperforming projects without elevating them to the level of the Strategic Information Technology Assessment and Review board. During the months in which the board meetings are scheduled, the Deputy Commissioner for Systems is to meet with staff prior to these meetings to

---

[16]The Clinger-Cohen Act (40 U.S.C. §§ 11301-11331) provides a framework for effective IT management that encompasses systems integration planning and investment.

prepare to address concerns about investments that may be raised during the meetings. If concerns are raised at the meeting, the Deputy Commissioner for Systems is to provide information about these investments. In addition, the Strategic Information Technology Assessment and Review board is to receive investment profiles on the status of each of the agency's major IT investments. These profiles should include reports on actual and expended work years, cost, schedule, and any variances.

During the *evaluation* phase, the Capital Planning and Investment Control guide calls for the Deputy Commissioner for Systems to conduct post-implementation reviews on projects that have been completed and deployed for at least 3 months. The purpose of these reviews is to compare actual project results against planned results in order to assess performance and identify areas where future decision making can be improved.

GAO and Other Reviews Have Highlighted the Importance for SSA to Strategically Plan for Modernizing Its Aging Legacy Systems

Since 2007, we and others have issued a number of reports highlighting various IT challenges that SSA has faced. These reports, collectively, have stressed the need for SSA to strategically plan to modernize its IT systems and infrastructure.

The National Research Council of the National Academies reported in 2007[17] that SSA's COBOL-oriented applications were very expensive to write, debug, and maintain. It concluded that SSA faced significant ongoing change and that it should embrace change as a constant, regularly evaluate emerging trends in areas such as technology and business practices, evaluate the societal attitudes and expectations of its various user communities, and institutionalize the formulation of strategies for addressing these trends. The report also stated that SSA's organizational structure does not support the establishment of a strategic focus in electronic services that is sufficiently high-level and broad-based. The report recommended, among other things, that SSA make an unambiguous, strategic commitment to electronic services as part of its

---

[17]The National Research Council is a private, nonprofit research organization dedicated to helping shape sound policies, inform public opinion, and advance the pursuit of science, engineering, and medicine. It is part of the National Academies. L. Osterweil, L. Millett, and J. Winston (editors), *Social Security Administration Electronic Service Provision: A Strategic Assessment*, National Academies Press (Washington, D.C.: August 2007).

long-term service delivery strategy, placing a central emphasis on electronic services that encompass timely and up-to-date information for users, partners, and beneficiaries.

In September 2008, we reported[18] that SSA had executed a majority of key IT investment management practices. However, the critical process of providing oversight was not being fully executed. Further, we reported that a gap existed in the agency's management of its IT in that more than half of its budget—its acquisition budget—was not being overseen as part of the agency's current investment management process. We made recommendations related to strengthening the investment board's role and responsibilities and improving post-implementation reviews, among other things. SSA agreed with our recommendation regarding the need to perform post-implementation reviews, and stated that it planned to evaluate quantitative measures and lessons learned for improving the select, control, and evaluate processes; however, it did not do so.

In January 2009, we reported[19] that increases in retirement and disability filings, along with ongoing and expected increases in retirements of SSA's most experienced staff, posed difficult challenges for the agency in meeting future service delivery needs. We recommended that the agency take steps to address these challenges and develop a plan to describe how it would deliver quality service in the future while managing the growing work demands with constrained resources. SSA disagreed with our recommendation to prepare a detailed plan to address future service delivery needs. Rather, it commented that it continually plans for the future and has been long aware of escalating disability and retirement claims workloads.

In September 2009, we reported[20] that while SSA's existing IT infrastructure effectively supported its current outgoing and incoming

---

[18]GAO, *Information Technology: SSA Has Taken Key Steps for Managing Its Investments, but Needs to Strengthen Oversight and Fully Define Policies*, GAO-08-1020 (Washington, D.C.: Sept. 12, 2008).

[19]GAO, *Social Security Administration: Service Delivery Plan Needed to Address Baby Boom Retirement Challenges*, GAO-09-24 (Washington, D.C.: Jan. 9, 2009).

[20]GAO, *Information Technology: Social Security Administration's Data Exchanges Support Current Programs, but Better Planning Is Needed to Meet Future Demands*, GAO-09-966 (Washington, D.C.: Sept. 16, 2009).

electronic data exchange environment, the agency and its data exchange partners anticipated that the demand for these exchanges would grow and that the methods for exchanging data would become more complex. However, SSA had not performed the detailed analyses needed to project the workload and performance requirements of a future data exchange environment. In addition, we found that the agency's target enterprise architecture[21] environment did not address specific business and technical requirements for supporting its data exchange program. We recommended that SSA conduct the analyses needed to define requirements for delivering data exchange services to its partners in the future and use the results of these analyses to update its target architecture. SSA agreed with these recommendations; however, in July 2011, the agency told us that while project proposals were submitted to address shortcomings in the information exchange and Social Security number verification processes, including a complete redesign of the software used for Social Security number and benefit verifications, funding constraints limited the agency's progress toward the comprehensive assessment and subsequent improvement of information exchange and verification systems.

The Inspector General for SSA reported[22] in May 2010 that the agency lacked a long-term, comprehensive strategic project plan for converting critical databases to a commercial product. The Inspector General also reported that while SSA successfully completed the first phase of its Master Data Access Method file management system to the DB2 Data Base Management System, the project implementation strategy was not efficient because the strategy resulted in a less-than-optimal database design. The Inspector General recommended that SSA establish a long-term, comprehensive strategic plan for the project and related major IT initiatives, including the project's estimated costs for all resources, schedules for all tasks, and performance goals for the entire life cycle.

---

[21]An enterprise architecture is a blueprint, or road map, of an agency's current and planned operating and systems environment, as well as an IT investment plan for transitioning between the two.

[22]Office of the Inspector General, Social Security Administration, *Conversion of the Social Security Administration's Legacy File Management System*, A-14-09-19097 (Baltimore, Md.: May 2010).

In June 2010, SSA's Future Systems Technology Advisory Panel[23] reported that given the projected workload increases because of the number of individuals retiring over the next two decades and other demographic trends, electronic self-service appears to be the only solution that will enable SSA to process future transaction volumes and provide outstanding service to SSA constituents, including "baby boomer" retirees and applicants for disability.[24] The panel made a series of recommendations to SSA, including that the agency move to an electronic customer self-service model with the goal of moving transactions to the Internet each year until 90 percent of the business with SSA takes place online and establish electronic service delivery as a strategic goal for all employees.

In March 2011, the Social Security Advisory Board reported[25] that SSA should initiate a long-range strategic planning process to serve as a guide for future program and systems development, and that leadership should address an immediate need to develop a longer-range vision statement and implementation strategy (beyond the 2-year planning window that the Office of Systems leadership stated it had used). According to the report, this strategy should aim to fundamentally improve service delivery and customer service by being able to support portable technologies, eliminate unnecessary complexity, provide for real-time data availability, and support effective interagency information sharing and one-stop service delivery. To ensure success by 2020, the board stated that SSA must, among other things, establish a systems modernization plan that will move the agency to a modern technology platform and support enhanced service delivery options.

[23]The Future Systems Technology Advisory Panel was established by the SSA Commissioner in February 2008. The mission of the panel was to provide independent advice and recommendations on the future of systems technology and electronic services at SSA 5 to 10 years into the future. The panel was terminated by the Commissioner on January 9, 2012, because of budgetary constraints.

[24]Future Systems Technology Advisory Panel, *Re-imagining Social Security* (June 2010).

[25]Social Security Administration Advisory Board, *A Vision of the Future for the Social Security Administration* (Washington, D.C.: March 2011). The Social Security Advisory Board is an independent bipartisan board created by Congress and appointed by the President and Congress to provide advice to the President, Congress, and the Commissioner of Social Security on matters related to the Social Security and Supplemental Security Income programs.

In April 2011, the SSA Inspector General noted that because the agency lacked complete, up-to-date documentation, its constantly evolving workforce might not be able to acquire an adequate understanding of a complex SSA cost analysis system, which could put continuity of operations at risk.[26] Specifically, the Inspector General's review found that SSA developed and updated the system's policies and procedures on a piecemeal basis and that the documents had not been comprehensively reviewed. Further, the Inspector General noted that key personnel had informally maintained institutional knowledge and that the agency lacked complete, up-to-date documentation and established processes. These weaknesses in system documentation could result in a situation where new employees would be challenged in understanding the inner workings of the cost analysis system. Thus, the Inspector General concluded that SSA's continuity of operations could be at risk.

Realignment of SSA's Office of the CIO

In June 2011, to maximize efficiency, SSA realigned CIO functional areas of the organization and associated personnel.[27] As part of this realignment, the Office of the Chief Information Officer was eliminated, and most of its CIO responsibilities, along with the IT budget, were reassigned to the Office of Systems. Specifically, the Offices of Innovation, Information Security, and Investment Management, as well as divisions of the Office of Vision and Strategy, were moved to the Office of Systems. According to the Deputy Commissioner for Systems, of 144 former CIO staff, 94 were reassigned to the Office of Systems. Of the remaining former CIO staff, 44 were assigned to component offices other than the Office of Systems, and 6 departed the agency. As a result, approximately 3,300 IT staff and contractors are now assigned to the Office of Systems.

Under the prior organizational structure, SSA's Office of the CIO and the Office of Systems had operated as distinct entities. In this regard, the CIO had headed the agency's investment review board, which met monthly to

---

[26]Office of the Inspector General for the Social Security Administration, *Cost Analysis System Background Report and Viability Assessment*, A-15-10-20149 (Baltimore, Md.: Apr. 11, 2011). The Cost Analysis System reviewed by the Office of the Inspector General is used by SSA's budget office to obtain workload and work year data to use in formulating and executing the budget and to measure aggregate productivity of SSA and its components.

[27]Commissioner Michael J. Astrue, Memorandum to Senior Staff, "Major Reorganization and Personnel Changes," June 24, 2011.

select and prioritize IT investments (IT projects and portfolios). Key duties of the CIO had included chairing the Strategic Information Technology Assessment and Review board, overseeing the review and approval of the annual IT budget, and ensuring that all IT acquisitions adhered to requirements of the Clinger-Cohen Act. From 2009 until the initiation of the realignment in 2011, the Office of the CIO had increased from approximately 30 staff to 144 staff, and added two offices—the Office of Innovation and the Office of Vision and Strategy—to support modernization efforts.

Prior to the realignment, the key duties of the Office of Systems were to manage the acquisition, development, and maintenance of all IT projects, formulate and execute the IT budget, provide to the CIO performance data for cost and schedule information for the investment review board review, and serve on the investment review board.

SSA Has Undertaken Numerous Modernization Efforts, but It Lacks Effective Measurements to Determine Progress

Since 2001, SSA has reported to OMB that it has spent nearly $11.9 billion on IT—more than $5 billion[28] of which has gone toward the development, modernization, and enhancement of its systems and capabilities. SSA's IT managers identified 120 initiatives undertaken from 2001 to 2011 that the agency considered to be significant investments in modernization.[29] According to the agency, these efforts have provided improvements such as enhanced work processes, automated notices to beneficiaries, and modifications to existing systems to accommodate legislative changes,[30] among other things. However, many identified projects remain to be completed for SSA to modernize its IT environment. Further, while OMB guidance[31] directs agencies to develop such tools, thus far, SSA has not fully established comprehensive performance measures and metrics to assess progress toward agency goals or performed post-implementation reviews, which would enable the agency to effectively measure and determine its progress in modernization. As a result, the agency cannot measure and report the effectiveness and efficiency of progress towards its goals for IT systems and capabilities.

---

[28]As previously noted, SSA was not required by OMB to account for DME and O&M spending for fiscal year 2001, and for fiscal years 2002 and 2003; the agency was only required to report DME and O&M for major projects. Thus this figure may be understated.

[29]SSA managers represented five major IT functional areas: Title II: Administering disability, old age, and survivor benefits; Title XVI: Administering Supplemental Security Income; Data Exchange: sending and receiving electronic information with third parties; Enumeration: Allocation and verification of Social Security numbers; and Disability: Determination, control, and tracking of disability claims. These projects do not represent all of SSA's initiatives over the 11-year time frame; only ones highlighted by these officials as key completed modernization efforts that provided process improvements, new functionalities, and/or new redesigned systems.

[30]An example of a modification to accommodate legislative changes was responding to American Recovery and Reinvestment Act of 2009 (Pub. L. No. 111-5, § 2201, Feb. 17, 2009) requirements by adapting the systems to provide a $250 payout to Social Security recipients.

[31]OMB, Circular A-130, Transmittal Memorandum No. 4, "Management of Federal Information Resources, 8. b (1)" (Washington, D.C.: Nov. 28, 2000).

GAO-12-495 Information Technology

SSA Modernization Efforts Have Yielded Improvements, but Major Efforts Are Still Under Way

As we have reported in prior work,[32] investments in modernizing IT can have a dramatically positive impact on an organization's performance. If managed effectively, these investments can vastly improve government performance and accountability. In addition, as discussed previously, SSA's enterprisewide Agency Strategic Plan states that the agency intends to modernize its IT environment by updating its data center infrastructure, incrementally modernizing its older software applications based on business opportunity and technical risk, and increasing the use of Web-based technologies to provide online public access to the agency's services.

SSA officials identified 120 initiatives undertaken from 2001 to 2011 that the agency considered to be significant investments in development, modernization, and enhancement. These comprise a subset of the hundreds of projects and modernization activities SSA undertakes yearly, which vary greatly in level of effort, scope, and cost and range from reengineering processes and developing new systems to enhancing and improving the functionality of existing systems. Of these 120 initiatives, more than two-thirds were for enhanced software or new functionality for legacy systems, while the remaining projects were aimed at moving from manual to online processes and developing new system software to reengineer processes, among other things.[33]

Key modernization initiatives completed by SSA from 2001 to 2011 affected all of the agency's main program areas. Examples of these are described below.

Reducing disability hearings backlogs was a major agency priority during the period from 2001 to 2011, and continues to be so going forward.[34] To respond to this priority, SSA's managers within the Office of Disability Systems described steps taken to create an electronic folder process in

---

[32]GAO, *Information Technology Management: Governmentwide Strategic Planning Performance Measurement and Investment Management Can Be Further Improved*, GAO-04-49 (Washington, D.C., Jan. 12, 2004).

[33]Office of Systems officials said that SSA does not keep track of projects according to whether a project is a modernization, redesign, or enhancement.

[34]SSA has reported progress toward eliminating its hearings-level backlog—defined as reducing the number of pending cases to SSA's target of 466,000. In March 2010, SSA reported that pending cases were down to 697,437 from 760,000 in fiscal year 2008.

order to replace the paper-based process field offices had to use in the past and improve hearings file access for persons representing disability applicants and beneficiaries. These projects included the following:

- The Disability Work Process, called eView. This project was to provide the capability to electronically view an applicant's folder, see the changes to that folder over time, and create a compact disc containing the files. The previous process required making a print copy of each file in the folder when requested, which generated significant issues, errors, and costs associated with a paper-based process.

- The Quick Disability Determinations project. This project introduced a computer program that screens cases for faster disability determinations for the most severely disabled individuals. This allows cases to be "fast tracked," reducing case processing time.

- The Electronic Access for Appointed Representatives project. This provides for Internet access to "folders" of information on hearings to determine eligibility for disability benefits.[35] Previously, appointed representatives[36] had to visit an SSA field office to request a compact disc with the hearings folder information. This project improved access to the folders for appointed representatives and reduced workloads for field representatives.

Also during this period, the Office of Retirement and Survivors Insurance Systems took steps to improve outdated SSA legacy systems and respond to legislation or other legal changes that required added functionality to systems. SSA officials described the following efforts:

---

[35]The disability determination process begins when an SSA staff member determines whether a claimant meets the program's nonmedical eligibility criteria. A claimant denied at this level may ask the disability determination service for a reconsideration of its finding. If the claim is denied again, the claimant may appeal to SSA's Office of Disability Adjudication and Review, where an administrative law judge will review the claim during a hearing and render a decision. A claimant whose appeal is subsequently denied may request a review by SSA's Appeals Council and, if denied again, may file suit in federal court.

[36]Disability claimants may be represented in their interactions with SSA by an attorney or a non-attorney. Claimants who choose to use a representative must appoint that individual and notify SSA of this appointment. A representative may act on a claimant's behalf in a number of ways, including getting information from the claimant's Social Security file.

- The Title II/Office of Retirement and Survivors Insurance Systems project. This project integrated standalone post-entitlement processes and improved field office efficiencies in interviewing applicants.

- Enabling a system to track attempts by fugitive felons to claim Supplemental Security Income benefits.[37]

- Modifying the benefit payment system to reflect a cost-of-living adjustment of zero along with a simultaneous increase in other benefits.[38]

- Processing a one-time payment of $250 to Social Security beneficiaries as part of the American Recovery and Reinvestment Act.[39]

- Integrated iClaims, which is an Internet application that allows the public to apply online for, among other programs, Title II initial benefits. Previously, applicants had to visit or call a field office, and SSA field personnel had to key in the applicant information manually.

- Completed Title II conversion from a non-relational database to a more modern industry-standard database, improving data access and information sharing.

SSA systems managers from the Office of Applications and Supplemental Security Income described projects designed to improve the overall effectiveness and responsiveness of the Title XVI process. This included

---

[37]According to SSA officials, this project required the agency to track the status of individuals who self-reported their felon status. SSA needed to make modifications to the database to account for this type of self reporting and help ensure that these individuals were not provided benefits payments.

[38]This is referred to as the "no COLA" (cost-of-living adjustment) project. According to SSA officials, while there was no cost-of-living adjustment in 2009, during that year Medicare premiums were increased. This complicated the variable process because some beneficiaries were not given a rate increase but were still subject to Medicare Part B premium increases. Agency officials stated that this created more work than would be expected, and because its software code was prepared for applying a COLA, SSA programmers had never performed a "no COLA." SSA also had to test the adjustment to make sure it was not inappropriately impacting claimants.

[39]The American Recovery and Reinvestment Act of 2009 is an economic stimulus package. Pub. L. No. 111-5, § 2201, Feb. 17, 2009.

efforts to modernize its large legacy databases and data sharing and efforts to enhance the claims process. Examples include the following:

- SSA's computation software was modified to allow for automatic calculation of attorneys' fees in order to avoid over- and underpayments.[40]

- The electronic death registration process was enhanced. This project allows a state to verify the name and Social Security number of the decedent prior to sending the report of death to SSA's system. Prior to this system enhancement, state agencies used a paper-based process for reporting deaths, and this initiative improved the timeliness of obtaining death notices in order to avoid improper payments to deceased persons.

- A Web application was developed that enables access to data from multiple systems, provides field office personnel instructions, and guides them through the claims process.

SSA officials also described initiatives in the area of electronically exchanging data with external partners. These included the following projects:

- Real-time verification of Social Security numbers for Title II and Title XVI benefits information. This initiative changed a batch-processing approach to an online process, improving the timeliness of data provided to state partners.

- Allowing state bureaus of vital statistics to verify the Social Security numbers of deceased persons using the Internet. Prior to implementation of this system, this process was paper based. The online access improved states' ability to verify decedent Social Security numbers and reduced the labor required of SSA's field office staff in looking up these numbers and advising states over the phone.

---

[40]This project was undertaken to reduce overpayments and underpayments to attorneys involved in Title II or Title XVI claimant representation and was an enhancement to the systems' attorney fee work processes. According to SSA officials, this project involved altering SSA's computation software to automatically calculate fees/payments to attorneys.

- Deployment of a consent-based Web service to allow machine-to-machine information sharing with banks, credit bureaus, and other private businesses to verify names and Social Security numbers in SSA's databases. This improved the timeliness of SSA data availability to private-sector businesses.

Finally, SSA noted efforts it undertook to streamline and secure its process for administering Social Security cards:

- Conversion of the Social Security number (enumeration) application to a more modern programming language.

- Conversion of the Social Security numbers' master file data base, called NUMIDENT, to a more modern industry-standard database, DB2. The NUMIDENT database was the first master file in SSA to be converted to this more modern database.

- Changes to Social Security cards to safeguard against counterfeiting, tampering, alteration, and theft. To respond to the Intelligence Reform and Terrorism Prevention Act,[41] SSA complied with relevant requirements of the Act by implementing the use of counterfeit resistant card stock, among other features added to the physical card, such as a cycle date and control number.

- Replacement of legacy dot matrix printers that printed Social Security cards with more modern hardware. According to officials, this replacement was necessary because these printers were obsolete and parts could not be purchased for them anymore. The replacement of outmoded printers improved system performance and maintenance and downtime issues associated with the obsolete hardware.

In addition to these initiatives, SSA has undertaken a project[42] to support its National Computer Center's IT architecture at a different location in order to enable restoration of IT operations within 1 day in the event of a

---

[41]Pub. L. No. 108-458, § 7213, Dec. 17, 2004.

[42]According to SSA, this was a major initiative called Information Technology Operational Assurance, which included building a fully provisioned second co-processing data center, positioning the agency for timely service continuity in the event of loss of either of the two data centers with a 1-day recovery time objective. Also, according to the SSA, this initiative includes continual data replication and very high-speed connection between the two centers.

disaster. The goals of the project were 100 percent IT operations foundational capacity, including mainframes, uninterrupted power supply, security, and operations space. This was to ensure continuity of systems operations and personnel, continuous processing of a portion of SSA's critical and non-critical workloads, and backup of the IT assets of the National Computer Center, and to enable either center to quickly assume the workload of the other. The initiative began in March 2005, and SSA requested about $125 million over 5 years to implement it.

Major Efforts Are Currently Under Way to Continue the Modernization of SSA's IT Environment

While the 120 key modernization efforts completed from 2001 to 2011 have improved SSA's ability to deliver services, the agency has several major initiatives still under way to continue the modernization of its IT environment. Specifically, in order to help meet its enterprisewide agency strategic goal of strengthening SSA's workforce and infrastructure and further enhancing its online services as established in its 2013–2016 Agency Strategic Plan, the agency intends to further improve and modernize its IT systems and capabilities in several key areas, including modernizing its Title II system, streamlining its disability program databases, enhancing telecommunications equipment, and completing its infrastructure changes to restore IT operations in the event of a disaster. To support these goals and other initiatives, the agency has described several major modernization efforts it has under way:

- Complete the conversion from the agency's Master Data Access Method database system to an industry standard and more modern database management system to provide more functionality and flexibility for processing future workloads. The Master Data Access Method database was developed in the early 1980s and was written in a programming language that is no longer widely used, which, when combined with the system's complexity, makes it difficult to train or recruit new programmers. This project, which is currently under way, will reduce system maintenance costs and allow the agency the ability to more readily and easily respond to changing program and technology needs. The agency has converted from this system to a more modern database for its Social Security number and earning files and is in the process of converting the Supplemental Security Record file; it plans to convert one of its largest files, the Master Beneficiary Records file, beginning in 2012. SSA plans to complete the conversion of the system to a more modern database system in fiscal year 2014.

- Transition from its legacy Title II system for processing about 9 million initial retirement and survivors' claims and about 800 to 850 million post-entitlement transactions annually. The existing Title II system consists of multiple applications implemented as early as the 1960s, some of which have not been updated and are still functioning as originally designed. In addition, the system contains redundancies in data processing and storage. The agency's vision is to create a single, unified Title II system that integrates initial and post-entitlement actions without redundant application code. This transition would provide conversions of key COBOL-based applications to more efficient, Web-based technology. To carry this out, SSA has outlined about 30 modernization projects that it plans to execute on an incremental and continuous basis.

- Streamline operations and reduce duplication in disability databases and allow for more efficient maintenance. The objective of the Disability Case Processing System is to transition the agency from multiple and fragmented applications—used by its state Disability Determination Services—to a modern, common case processing system. The current state disability systems are complex and constrain the agency's capability to make required updates in response to regulations, laws, and business rules. Maintenance and upgrades are complicated by the need to correspond to 54 independent state systems. The transition to a new common system across all state disability components is planned to allow SSA to accomplish software updates more efficiently and provide interfaces with SSA field offices. Modernization of the disability IT environment is also intended to help move the agency toward integrating the entire claims process from start to finish, and ultimately contribute to significant improvements for the entire disability process. SSA plans to complete this project by the end of fiscal year 2016.

- Enhance and refresh telecommunications equipment and provide ongoing improvement of connectivity and bandwidth for data, voice, and video communications. This project is intended, in part, to reduce SSA's hearing backlog by enabling video hearings between administrative law judges, claimants, and representatives from across the country. The agency plans to complete this project by the end of fiscal year 2015.

- Medicare Support Activities. This program provides the IT services supporting enhancements to SSA's Medicare initiatives, including changes required by the Patient Protection and Affordable Care Act.[43] Systems enhancements are intended to improve the process that verifies the name, Social Security number, and data on Medicare earnings reports.

SSA officials noted that the agency needs to overcome several challenges to improve its aging legacy systems and system capabilities. These include

- planning for system changes within a single fiscal-year budget cycle, a practice that limits the agency's ability to make long-range modernization plans;

- devoting resources to system maintenance because of the large quantities of legacy code in systems, along with the loss of subject-matter experts and inadequate documentation of legacy software; and

- diverting resources from long-term modernization efforts to deal with new legislative requirements, such as the Patient Protection and Affordable Care Act, judicial determinations, and collaboration with outside partners, such as states.

SSA Has Not Fully Established Performance Measures for Determining Modernization Progress

Even as SSA has recognized challenges for the efforts it has planned or undertaken to modernize IT, the agency has not fully established quantifiable and comprehensive performance measures to gauge the progress of investments and to determine how they contribute to the overall goals of the agency's mission. As we have reported, comprehensive performance measures and post-implementation reviews are essential for gauging the progress and benefits of investments in IT.[44] By establishing such measures and then monitoring actual-versus-expected performance,[45] an organization can better understand progress,

---

[43]Pub. L. No. 111-148, § 10323, Mar. 23, 2010. This act made changes to Medicare Part A and Part B coverage. The act provided Medicare Part A coverage, along with eligibility for Part B and D, to individuals exposed to certain health hazards within areas federally determined to represent an environmentally based public health emergency.

[44]GAO-04-49.

[45]Monitoring actual-versus-expected performance is comparing the actual result with the target measure at the major initiative level (which may be a program made up of multiple projects or a single project).

as well as the need for any corrective actions, in achieving its IT strategic goals. The Paperwork Reduction Act requires federal agencies to establish performance measures that depict how effectively the management of information resources, which include information technology, is supporting their mission needs.[46] Further, OMB provides agencies with guidance on developing performance measures for IT projects in four management areas (mission and business results, processes and activities, customer results, and technology).[47]

For fiscal year 2010, SSA identified at least one performance measure in each of the four management areas for 14 of its 17 major IT modernization investments.[48] For example, for the technology area of reliability and availability, SSA identified a measure to reduce the return-to-service time after a telephone system outage—from 600 minutes on its legacy systems to 110 minutes on installed systems—for its telephone replacement investment supporting the agency goal to "Improve Our Retiree and Other Core Services." In another example, for the area of mission and business results, the agency identified a measure to increase the number of participating providers exchanging medical evidence within its Health Information Technology investment–from 4 to 12 in fiscal year 2010–to support its agency goal to "Eliminate Our Hearings Backlog and Prevent Its Recurrence."

For 3 of the 17 investments—the Disability Case Processing System, Infrastructure Office Automation and the Medicare Modernization Act[49] investments—SSA did not identify any measures in one of the four

---

[46]The Clinger-Cohen Act also requires agencies to establish performance measures, such as those related to how IT contributes to program productivity, efficiency, and effectiveness, and to monitor the actual-versus-expected performance of those measures. Further, to be effective, as part of the Federal Enterprise Architecture, agencies should include a performance reference model in order to provide a means for using an agency's enterprise architecture to measure the success of IT investments and their impact on strategic outcomes.

[47]Office of Management and Budget, Executive Office of the President of the United States, *Federal Enterprise Architecture: Consolidated Reference Model Document*, version 2.3 (Washington, D.C.: October 2007).

[48]These measurements for fiscal year 2010 were reported in SSA's 2012 OMB exhibit 300 budget submission.

[49]Medicare Prescription Drug, Improvement, and Modernization Act of 2003, Pub. L. No. 108-173, Dec. 8, 2003.

management areas. Specifically, the agency did not provide any metrics in the area of mission and business results for the disability system or for the area of processes and activities for the agency's Infrastructure Office Automation and Medicare Modernization Act investments. SSA officials stated that for the disability system, they had identified a metric in this area, but removed it from their report to OMB because the contract for the project had not been awarded. They further stated that they included the metric in the following year's report when the contract was awarded. However, this is inconsistent with the use of metrics to gauge progress since identifying them allows agencies to be held accountable for results. For the Infrastructure Office Automation investment, officials stated that OMB does not require metrics in the processes and activities area for infrastructure investments. Nevertheless, this investment has process- and activity-oriented goals,[50] and having such a measure could help determine if the project is meeting goals. Finally, for the Medicare Modernization Act investment, the agency reported that the investment was a modernization of the program, not of IT. However, while the investment was to modernize a program, it was supported by an IT initiative to build upon existing software to ensure that the new business processes are integrated into SSA's overall business process. As such, this IT enhancement should be measured. Subsequently, the agency acknowledged that a metric was not provided specifically for this IT investment in fiscal year 2010, but stated that a metric for a different segment of the modernization program also applied to this effort. Officials further stated that this metric needed to be improved and revised it in a later submission. However, it is important to establish metrics prior to implementing the initiative to monitor actual-versus-expected performance and ensure adequate oversight.

In addition, the measures that SSA did develop for the 17 investments were not comprehensive in that they did not always (1) identify how each investment is to contribute to expected benefits; (2) include measures of the investments' effectiveness in meeting goals, requirements, or mission results; or (3) provide the means for measuring progress toward specific modernization goals.

---

[50]According to SSA's project overview submitted to OMB, the Office Automation Infrastructure project's goal was to improve retiree and other core services and the speed and quality of SSA's disability processing in several specific, measurable ways.

- SSA's measures for its IT investments often overlapped and did not always identify how each investment was to contribute to expected benefits. The Government Performance and Results Act requires agencies to develop performance plans for their program activities, including objective, quantifiable, and measurable goals for the program and how each program activity is to contribute to that goal.[51] However, in a number of cases,[52] SSA identified a measure that applied to multiple investments, but did not explain how, or to what extent, the individual investments would contribute to expected program results or outputs. For example, four investments—the Telecommunications Infrastructure, Data Center Infrastructure, Automation Infrastructure, and Ready Retirement investments—identified a measure of processing 100 percent of retirement and survivor claims receipts up to the budgeted level, but did not establish an "efficiency" goal of this business activity and identify the extent to which each specific investment would contribute to achieving this efficiency. In another example, the agency established a goal of improving the speed and quality of its disability process and a corresponding measure of minimizing average processing time for initial disability claims. This measure was associated with five of SSA's investments—Intelligent Disability, Disability Determination Services Automation, Disability Claims Processing System, Health IT, and Telecommunications Infrastructure—but the agency did not identify how or to what extent these individual investments would contribute to this goal. More detailed performance information could include capturing the extent of applicable legal requirements or manual processes that the project has fully automated. Without performance measures that include this information, it will be unclear whether or to what extent SSA's modernization investments are contributing to its goals.

---

[51]Pub. L. No. 103-62, § 4(b), Aug. 3, 1993, 107 Stat. 285, 287 (codified at 31 U.S.C. § 1115(b)).

[52]For the 17 investments, we found that about 40 percent, or 42 out of 104, of the measures identified by SSA were applied to multiple investments. Each of the 17 investments could have measures in the four areas, as well as sub-measures under each area. We did, however, exclude from our identified 42 measures selected measures that were appropriately applied to multiple investments, such as disaster recovery and continuity of operation efforts (for example, the reduction or elimination of single points of failure measure).

- SSA did not always include measures of the IT investment's effectiveness in meeting goals or requirements. OMB's Federal Enterprise Architecture Performance Reference Model identifies both effectiveness and efficiency measures as key to evaluating an IT investment.[53] Effectiveness measures include the investment's impact on the performance of the processes and how it contributes to mission results (referred to as "technology effectiveness"), while efficiency measures key elements of the system's performance, such as the user accessibility and improved technical capabilities. Other key measures include technology costs and quality assurance.[54] While SSA defined at least one technology performance measure for each investment, these measures primarily addressed technology efficiencies and reliability and availability of the systems, rather than cost, quality, and effectiveness. Specifically, 15 of the 17 investments had measures for efficiencies and reliability and availability, but only 3 investments had measures for technology effectiveness, 1 for quality assurance, and none for technology costs. In spite of not defining technology effectiveness measures for most of these investments, SSA reported that it expects to achieve key benefits from these investments in technology effectiveness, efficiency, and costs. For example, while SSA reported that its major Title II investment will provide various efficiency and cost benefits, such as a reduction in internal work hand-offs, fewer calls and office visits from beneficiaries, less costly maintenance, and a reduction in risk through consolidating systems, it only provided reliability and availability measures for this investment. The use of cost, efficiency, effectiveness, and quality assurance measures for its investments would allow the agency to capture critical elements of performance needed to determine if an investment is achieving the expected benefits and supporting agency mission needs.

- SSA did not develop measures for determining progress in meeting its modernization goals. As discussed above, SSA's goals for its modernization efforts include introducing online services that require less human intervention, reducing the overall growth rate of

---

[53]As stated in OMB's Federal Enterprise Architecture, the Performance Reference Model framework provides common output measurements. The guidance identifies key measures of performance directly relating to an IT investment, such as measures of efficiency and measures of effectiveness.

[54]Quality assurance measures include the extent to which technology supports capability requirements and complies with standards and best practices.

infrastructure costs, removing older and more costly applications, and reducing risk through consolidating systems. However, SSA has not defined measures for its investments that describe progress toward modernization goals. For example, SSA reported measures for its Title II Redesign Initiative—which includes modernization activities—such as achieving the target percentages of retirement claims filed online and of individuals rating their experience with SSA services as "excellent," "very good," or "good," but it has not defined modernization-related measures. Modernization-related measures could include, for example, the percentage of legacy applications redesigned, the number of lines of application code reduced by consolidation, or the cost of code maintenance. Similarly, SSA has not developed modernization-related measures for its Medicare Modernization Act initiative, instead establishing measures for the satisfaction rating of customers using the Internet Medicare Part D Subsidy Application[55] and the percentage of individuals who do business with SSA rating the overall services as "excellent," "very good," or "good." Instead, fully establishing modernization-related measures would help demonstrate how the modernization effort contributes to achieving the expected benefits.

In discussing this matter, SSA IT managers and budget officials stated that there are many factors that contribute to the success of the agency's performance measures, and that any attempt to quantify the contribution of each activity would be resource-intensive and highly subjective. The officials further stated that, in their view, it is sufficient to clearly demonstrate achieving a goal and that there are specific program or project measures that do not roll up to the high-level agency measures. While we agree that developing high-level goals and demonstrating that these goals are met is important to measuring progress, without fully establishing comprehensive and quantifiable measures of how individual projects are contributing to those goals, SSA cannot know whether it is investing in the appropriate mix of modernization projects. Moreover, it may be limited in its ability to make well-informed decisions about redirecting or terminating projects that may not be contributing to these goals or experiencing performance problems. Further, the lack of such

---

[55]The Medicare Part D Extra Help program helps Medicare beneficiaries with limited income and resources pay for prescription drug coverage. Eligible beneficiaries receive subsidized premiums, deductibles, and copayments. Potential beneficiaries can apply for the program using the SSA i1020, which is an online application on SSA's website.

comprehensive and quantifiable measures for individual projects limits the ability of oversight bodies, both internal and external, to understand the effectiveness and efficiency of SSA's efforts.

SSA Has Not Conducted Post-Implementation Reviews to Assess Projects

OMB's *Circular A-130* establishes requirements for conducting a post-implementation review of an IT project or system, which includes confirming the extent to which planned benefits were achieved, determining the cost-effectiveness of the project, and identifying lessons learned and opportunities to improve modernization-related elements.[56] Moreover, SSA guidance requires post-implementation reviews to be conducted 3 to 12 months after a system has become operational.[57]

We reported in 2008, however, that SSA had not adequately implemented key practices associated with performing post- implementation reviews and recommended that the agency evaluate quantitative measures during post-implementation reviews.[58] As noted earlier, SSA agreed with our recommendation.

Nonetheless, according to the Deputy Commissioner for Systems, SSA does not currently conduct post-implementation reviews for projects. Rather, the agency conducts post-release reviews, which briefly summarize whether users felt the project was adequately completed, effective management practices for broader use, and lessons learned. However, these reviews lack the critical elements of post-implementation reviews that could indicate how well a project has improved program performance. Further, in 2010, SSA's Inspector General found that, while SSA's post-implementation review policy met OMB requirements, the agency's post-release reviews did not fully comply with this policy and instead narrowly focused on validating service requirements. The report cited missing elements such as comparing estimated project costs to

---

[56]OMB, *Circular A-130*, Transmittal Memorandum No. 4, "Management of Federal Information Resources, 8. b (1)" (Washington, D.C.: Nov. 28, 2000).

[57]SSA annual capital planning and control guidance; see, for example, SSA, *Fiscal Year 2010 Information Technology Capital Planning and Investment Control Process* (Feb. 12, 2009).

[58] GAO-08-1020.

actual costs, evaluating mission and program impact, and evaluating customer and user satisfaction.[59]

SSA also reported using a project evaluation, called Project Success Verification, to assess completed initiatives. These evaluations focus on whether specific functionality was met. However, these verifications do not include critical elements of a post implementation review as required by OMB, including the validation of estimated costs and benefits, documentation of efficient management practices for broader use, documentation of lessons learned, or the redesign of oversight mechanisms and performance levels to incorporate lessons acquired during project implementation.

The Deputy Commissioner for Systems stated that SSA is planning to establish a post-implementation review process during fiscal year 2012. Until the agency implements post-implementation reviews that include critical elements as specified in OMB guidance, SSA will lack assurance that its modernization and other IT projects are delivering expected benefits at acceptable costs, and that it is making progress toward its goals.

SSA's Approach to IT Modernization Lacks Key Practices to Effectively Guide Efforts

Comprehensive strategic planning is essential for an organization to define what it seeks to accomplish, identify strategies to efficiently achieve the desired results, and effectively guide modernization efforts.[60] Key elements of strategic planning include an IT strategic plan and an enterprise architecture that together outline the agency's modernization goals, measures, and timelines. An IT strategic plan serves as an agency's vision and helps align its information resources with its business strategies and investment decisions. As such, it provides a high-level perspective of the goals and objectives, enabling an organization to prioritize how it allocates resources, proactively respond to changes, and communicate its IT vision and goals to management, oversight bodies, and external parties. The enterprise architecture helps to implement the strategic vision by providing a focused "blueprint" of the organization's

---

[59]SSA Office of the Inspector General, *The Social Security Administration's Post-Implementation Review Process*, A-14-10-30105 (June 2010).

[60]GAO, *Information Resources Management: Comprehensive Strategic Plan Needed to Address Mounting Challenges*, GAO-02-292 (Washington, D.C.: Feb. 22, 2002).

business processes and the technology that supports them, including descriptions of how the organization operates today, how it intends to operate in the future, and a plan for transitioning to the target state. The enterprise architecture also helps coordinate the concurrent development of IT systems in a manner that limits unnecessary duplication and increases the likelihood that systems will be interoperable.

However, SSA does not have an updated IT strategic plan to guide its modernization efforts or a complete enterprise architecture. Instead, SSA follows an approach that is driven by a short-term 2-year budget cycle and, according to the Deputy Commissioner for Systems, modernization efforts are determined based on an "opportunistic" approach.[61] Without a well-developed plan and long-range vision, the agency cannot be assured that its IT investments will match its strategic direction and effectively position the agency to cope with future challenges.

SSA Lacks a Current IT Strategic Plan to Guide Modernization Efforts

As we have previously reported, an IT strategic plan serves as an agency's vision or road map and helps align its information resources with its business strategies and investment decisions.[62] The plan includes the mission of the agency, key business processes, IT challenges, and guiding principles and should be aligned with the agency's overall strategic plan. The IT strategic plan enables an agency to consider the resources—including human, infrastructure, and funding—that are needed to manage, support, and pay for a project. For example, an IT strategic plan that identifies interdependencies within and across modernization projects helps to ensure that these are understood and managed, so that projects—and thus system solutions—are effectively integrated. *OMB Circular A-130, Management of Federal Information Resources*, requires agencies to develop such a plan to support the agency's overall enterprisewide strategic plan, provide a description of how IT-related activities are expected to help accomplish the agency's

---

[61]According to the Deputy Commissioner for Systems, this opportunistic approach allows SSA to take advantage of technology opportunities as they arise and as the agency's business needs evolve. It is driven by funding and allows workload characteristics and business needs to dictate IT investments.

[62]See GAO, *Information Technology: FDA Needs to Establish Key Plans and Processes for Guiding Systems Modernization Efforts*, GAO-09-523 (Washington, D.C.: June 2, 2009).

mission, and ensure that decisions are integrated with organizational planning and program decisions.

In summary, an IT strategic plan would provide a comprehensive picture of what the organization seeks to accomplish, identify the strategies it will use to achieve desired results, provide results-oriented goals and performance measures that permit it to determine whether it is succeeding, and describe interdependencies within and across projects so that these can be understood and managed.

SSA developed an IT strategic plan (which SSA refers to as its information resource management plan) in 2007 to guide its modernization efforts. However, the plan is outdated and may not be aligned with the agency's overall strategic plan. The Deputy Commissioner for Systems acknowledged that the plan needed to be revised. Specifically, because the IT strategic plan has not been updated since 2007, it contains elements that are no longer relevant to SSA's ongoing modernization efforts, as the following examples illustrate:

- The plan's discussion of the agency's capital planning and investment control process does not include a key component of its current process—the application portfolio management program. This tool is to be used to inventory and determine the health of the agency's software applications.

- The plan does not include SSA's nine portfolio vision statements.[63] These vision statements, according to Office of Systems officials, identify initiatives that support the agency's high-level business priorities.

- The plan identifies a key project to establish a disaster recovery capability at a secondary computing center; however, as noted earlier, this project has largely been completed.

- The plan does not reflect current information security requirements. Specifically, as of August 2010, agencies are required to monitor the

---

[63]The nine areas for which SSA established portfolio vision statements are: core services, cross-cutting (i.e., IT capabilities that support and enable core business functions across the enterprise), disability process, hearings process, high-performing workforce, program integrity, savings and solvency, SSA infrastructure, and Social Security number process.

security of their systems on a continuous basis.[64] However, SSA's plan calls for doing so every 3 years.

- The plan states that SSA's modernization efforts are driven by its enterprise architecture. While SSA has developed aspects of an enterprise architecture, it has not developed an enterprise gap analysis that would identify steps to transition from the current to the future architecture environment. Instead, agency officials told us that SSA's process is currently driven by opportunities for modernization that are identified by its IT Strategic Information Technology Assessment and Review board.

- IT staffing needs, as addressed in the plan, are only projected through fiscal year 2010.

Further, while SSA's enterprisewide Agency Strategic Plan was completed in 2008, the IT strategic plan was not updated and, as a result, may not be aligned with the Agency Strategic Plan. Based on OMB guidance, SSA should have updated the IT strategic plan and ensured that it aligns with the Agency Strategic Plan. Consequently, since 2008, the agency may have been making investments in IT projects and modernization efforts without the full benefit and guidance of an IT strategic plan that is aligned with the vision and goals set out in the Agency Strategic Plan.

Moreover, in February 2012, SSA issued a new Agency Strategic Plan to cover fiscal years 2013 to 2016. In this plan, SSA identified IT as one of the key foundational elements to achieving success in meeting the agencywide goals. This highlights the importance of SSA developing a current IT strategic plan, with detailed milestones and resources that align with agency strategic goals to effectively guide modernization efforts. In March 2012, SSA's Office of Systems officials stated that the agency was in the process of updating its IT strategic plan and expected to issue one in early 2012. However, as of mid-March 2012, SSA had not provided us with an updated agency-approved version of the plan.

---

[64]See U.S. Department of Commerce, National Institute of Standards and Technology, *Recommended Security Controls for Federal Information Systems and Organizations*, Special Publication 800-53, revision 3 (Gaithersburg, Md., August 2009).

In the absence of an updated IT strategic plan, SSA has relied on a number of program activities to guide IT modernization efforts. However, these activities are based on the short-term budget cycles and are not developed in the context of a long-term strategic plan with detailed steps and milestones to specifically guide modernization projects:

- SSA has established an application portfolio management program to determine the health of software applications, which can be used to identify and prioritize IT modernization investments during the annual Capital Planning and Investment Control process to manage its in-house software development projects. While these prioritization decisions, are, in part, based on what applications need to be enhanced or replaced because of the technical risk of failure, SSA IT officials acknowledged that these efforts are driven by the 2-year budget cycle, and resources may be redirected away from multi-year projects to accommodate immediate needs. Specifically, according to SSA's IT investment management officials, the agency must balance its modernization efforts with other needs based on limited resources.

- SSA has developed IT portfolio vision statements that are aligned with the agency's 2008 enterprisewide Agency Strategic Plan goals to prioritize and identify major IT initiatives and the high-level business outcomes for each initiative. According to Office of Systems officials, in March 2012, the agency plans to realign its portfolio vision statements to the current Agency Strategic Plan for 2013 to 2016. The Deputy Commissioner for Systems said the agency intends to gradually transition its applications by means of an "opportunistic"[65] approach that allows SSA to take advantage of technology opportunities as they arise and as the agency's business needs evolve. While taking advantage of technological advances and opportunities is essential to meet future business needs, to do so without an overall framework and detailed IT strategic plan could increase the risks that SSA will not make the best use of its IT

---

[65]SSA uses such terms to define its gradual approach to balance modernization with other business needs as opportunities arise and based on funding and business needs. For example, SSA plans to continue using both its mainframe and COBOL software, but will gradually transition its applications away from COBOL on an "opportunistic and evolutionary" basis. To do this, Java software will be used to build new core online applications, whether they are standalone on distributed platforms or front-end additions to existing legacy applications.

investments and may ultimately hinder the agency's efficiency and effectiveness in modernization efforts.

- SSA also prepares what the agency refers to as "pocket planners" to assist the portfolio teams in overseeing approved projects during the agency's annual IT Strategic Information Technology Assessment and Review board process. Pocket planners provide high-level information on portfolio projects, briefly describing the initiative and the functions the project is intended to perform. These planners also note dependencies with other projects or organizations and note, if appropriate, that the project is a high priority. While the pocket planners allow the portfolio team to review the current projects under way in the portfolio, the planners do not provide key elements, such as the project's risks, challenges, how to gauge progress, the specific work remaining, or the expected costs. Pocket planners also are missing key elements that would be included in an IT strategic plan— such as a comprehensive assessment of resources, including human, infrastructure, and funding needed to manage, support and pay for a project—and do not provide a foundation for realizing an enterprisewide strategic vision.

Without an updated IT strategic plan that sets forth a long-term vision and the intermediary steps that are needed to guide the agency, SSA may not effectively prioritize investments or use the best mix of limited resources to move toward its longer-term agencywide goals. Specifically, such a plan would help the agency proactively respond to budget fluctuations and other changes by enabling it to prioritize the allocation of resources in light of established goals and strategies. In the absence of a current IT strategic plan that is informed by SSA's most recent strategic goals, there remains a risk that IT investments may not be aligned with the agency's current priorities and modernization progress toward those goals may be uncertain.

SSA Has Developed an Enterprise Architecture, but Is Missing Key Components to Effectively Guide Modernization Activities

Like an IT strategic plan, an enterprise architecture is an important tool to help guide an organization's IT investments by ensuring that the planning and implementation of IT investments take full account of the business and technology environment in which the systems are to operate. A well-defined enterprise architecture thoroughly describes an organization's current and target states of IT systems and business operations and identifies the gaps and specific intermediary steps that the organization plans to take to achieve its target state. In short, an enterprise architecture is a blueprint for organizational change. OMB's guidance directs agencies to develop an enterprise architecture to guide IT strategic planning. We have also developed a framework for assessing and improving enterprise architecture management.[66] The framework is intended to provide a flexible benchmark against which to plan for and measure an enterprise architecture program. Not using an enterprise architecture can result in organizational operations and supporting technology infrastructures and systems that are duplicative, poorly integrated, unnecessarily costly to maintain and interface, and unable to respond quickly to shifting environmental factors.

SSA has developed an enterprise architecture for years 2011 through 2016 that captures certain foundational information about the current and target environments to assist in evolving existing information systems and developing new systems. In the architecture, the agency has identified current business processes (e.g., appeals) and described a vision and business outcomes for each enterprise segment (i.e., strategic objective portfolio). The vision includes (1) eliminating existing stove-piped application software and (2) reusing business services (e.g., accounting services and determination services) and IT services (e.g., authentication) to develop service-oriented architecture applications to replace aging online and back-office desktop applications. SSA has also developed an enterprise data model that can help guide the development of databases, and a technical framework and guidelines for software development.

Nevertheless, the enterprise architecture developed by SSA lacks important architecture content that would allow the agency to more effectively plan its investments to reach its vision of modernized systems and operations by its target date of 2016. According to federal CIO Council[67] guidance,[68] an agency that plans to implement a service-oriented architecture should develop a service-oriented architecture road map that, among other things, articulates the changes and growth in capabilities over time and provides a conceptual plan that is used as a basis for developing detailed project plans and allocating responsibilities

---

[66]GAO-10-846G.

[67]The federal CIO Council is the principal interagency forum to improve agency practices on such matters as the design, modernization, use, sharing, and performance of agency information resources.

[68]Federal CIO Council, *A Practical Guide to Federal Service Oriented Architecture*, version 1.1 (Washington, D.C.: June 2008).

to accomplish each of the activities. This guidance also states that agility must be purposely designed into the agency's enterprise architecture.

SSA reported that it has long supported the development of common software application components and services to encourage efficiency in developing new applications. For example, it stated that it has an inventory of common software application components, including 1,451 on-line and 1,201 batch components, and that it has recently developed 4 server-hosted enterprise services and 12 new mainframe-hosted enterprise services. In addition, SSA's enterprise architecture mentions the benefits of a service-oriented architecture, such as better agility in response to changes in the business environment and reduced costs to systems development and maintenance.

However, the agency has not developed a road map that articulates incremental changes and growth over time and that guides modernization activities to achieve such benefits. In addition, while SSA provides architectural standards and guidelines for designing a service-oriented architecture application, the agency's enterprise architecture does not include a service-oriented architecture conceptual plan that can be used as a basis for developing detailed project plans and allocating responsibilities to accomplish each of the activities. Such a plan is important since it provides direction and identifies key work that must be performed for SSA to incrementally achieve its vision of reusing service-oriented architecture services to quickly develop and maintain systems in response to changes in the business environment and reduce costs to systems development and maintenance. In addition, this would allow SSA to quickly respond to, for example, new legislation or court decisions without requiring laborious re-coding of subsystems.

Further, according to federal CIO Council guidance, an enterprise gap analysis should be the first step in developing an enterprise transition plan for migrating an architecture from the current environment to the future environment. Although SSA has developed aspects of a transition plan (e.g., a sequencing plan diagram) for migrating to the target environment, it has yet to develop an enterprise gap analysis. A gap analysis uses comparative analysis techniques to identify the differences between the current architecture and target architecture in terms of performance, business, data, services, technology, and security. The gap analysis is also important for determining the components that need to be changed and a comprehensive assessment of the state of the legacy systems, technology maturity, acquisition opportunities, and fiscal reality of the transition. According to SSA, its sequencing plan diagram is a result of the Strategic Information Technology Assessment and Review board process that involves discussions among business and IT staff to identify gaps and prioritize projects proposed for the current fiscal year. However, until a gap analysis is performed between the current and target architectures in terms of performance, business, information, applications, technologies, and security, the agency will lack important information that provides a basis for prioritization, integration, and synchronization across the spectrum of modernization activities.

In addition, OMB guidance[69] states that an agency's enterprise architecture should establish performance goals for each enterprise segment, including target performance measures, and the time frame to achieve the performance goals. OMB guidance also says that the enterprise transition plan should highlight the performance milestones that need to be met along the path to achieving the performance expected in the target environment. While SSA has described the performance of each strategic objective portfolio in the near term, it has not provided quantitative performance expectations for the target environment, including interim performance milestones that need to be met. Such information is important to identify performance improvement opportunities and measure the success of each strategic objective portfolio and its impact on the business outcomes.

Finally, OMB *Circular A-130* requires an agency's enterprise architecture to identify and document information flows and relationships. Specifically, an enterprise architecture should analyze the information used by the agency in its business processes, identify the information used, and describe the movement of the information. These information flows should also indicate where the information is needed and how the information is shared to support mission functions.

However, although SSA has developed data flow diagrams for systems such as the Supplemental Security Income Records Maintenance system certification and accreditation package, the agency has not developed information flows for the current and target environment from a business perspective. Specifically, the agency has not maintained information flows that identify the information used and the movement of the information

---

[69]Office of Management and Budget, *Enterprise Architecture Assessment Framework* v3.1 (June 2009).

among its business processes. Such information provides key input into identifying the points where information is exchanged; developing a broad, holistic view of the overall business information/data requirements; and defining a target enterprise application/service architecture that identifies the types of applications and services needed to support such requirements. The information flows are also important for establishing mutually understood data definitions and structures across business processes and enterprise segments. Without such data definitions and structures, there is an increased risk that SSA will need to invest significant time and resources to resolve heterogeneous data that vary in structure and semantics among multiple systems supporting different business processes and enterprise segments.

SSA systems officials acknowledge that the agency's enterprise architecture plan does not include a service-oriented architecture conceptual plan or a gap analysis. They stated that the agency's approach is to plan for developing new functionality or modernizing systems based on opportunities identified by the Strategic Information Technology Assessment and Review board process, instead of evaluating legacy systems to explore opportunities to create services or assessing the entire SSA enterprise from a central perspective.

While SSA's capital planning investment and control process allows for important input to the system needs and priorities, it is difficult to rely on agency personnel to manage and direct modernization efforts of such a magnitude as SSA's systems without a well-defined enterprise architecture. The federal CIO Council indicates that the agency's capital planning and investment control processes and enterprise architecture functions should be closely linked, both having a common focus: the effective and efficient management of IT investments. In this regard, a well-defined enterprise architecture would provide a strategic information base to support and inform the Strategic Information Technology Assessment and Review board's process, including providing information such as agencywide quantitative performance expectations for the current and future business and systems environment, as well as mutually understood data definitions and structures. This information could then be used as a basis for evaluating, among other things, the ability of proposed investments to address current and future agencywide business needs. Without a well-defined enterprise architecture that provides details on how SSA's modernization initiatives are to support its business processes and integrate with its existing infrastructure, SSA lacks additional assurance that these initiatives will effectively and efficiently support the agency's goals and mission.

CIO Realignment Allows for Effective Oversight and Management but Was Implemented without Adequate Planning or Updated Guidance

SSA has realigned the Office of the CIO's functions, responsibilities, and staff—with most of the office's responsibilities being transferred to the Office of Systems. Consequently, the Office of Systems now has the major responsibilities that federal law assigns to agency CIOs with regard to IT management. If appropriately implemented, the realignment could allow for effective oversight and management of the agency's IT modernization. However, while leading practices[70] stress the importance of major organizational realignments being supported by comprehensive analyses of the changes in roles and responsibilities, SSA did not make the realignment decisions based on a detailed analysis. The agency also has not completed updating its IT investment oversight guidance to reflect the realigned organization. Without an analysis of the realigned functions and how the newly assigned roles and responsibilities will carry out the former Office of CIO's functions, SSA lacks a basis by which the reassignment of duties can be assessed.

CIO Responsibilities Have Been Reassigned to the Office of the Deputy Commissioner for Systems

The Clinger-Cohen Act requires agency heads to designate a CIO with key responsibilities for managing an agency's IT resources.[71] The act supplemented the information technology management provisions of the Paperwork Reduction Act of 1995 with detailed requirements for IT capital planning and investment control and performance- and results-based management.[72] The Clinger-Cohen Act also gives CIOs related IT-management responsibilities, including providing advice and other assistance to the head of the agency on acquiring and managing IT,

---

[70]GAO, *OPM Retirement Modernization, Longstanding Information Technology Management Weaknesses Need to Be Addressed*, GAO-12-226T (Washington, D.C.: Nov. 15, 2011); *Results-Oriented Cultures: Implementation Steps to Assist Mergers and Organizational Transformations*, GAO-03-669 (Washington, D.C.: July 2, 2003); *Highlights of a GAO Forum: Mergers and Transformation: Lessons Learned for a Department of Homeland Security and Other Federal Agencies*, GAO-03-293SP (Washington, D.C.: Nov. 14, 2002); and *Veterans Affairs: Continued Focus on Critical Success Factors Is Essential to Achieving Information Technology Realignment*, GAO-07-844 (Washington, D.C.: June 15, 2007).

[71]44 U.S.C. § 3506(a)(2)(A), as amended by the Clinger-Cohen Act.

[72]Our review did not assess the extent to which SSA's CIO exercised all of the responsibilities given to CIOs by law, specifically 44 U.S.C. § 3506; 40 U.S.C. § 11315. For more information on the CIO's full role and responsibilities, see GAO, *Federal Chief Information Officers: Opportunities Exist to Improve Role in Information Technology Management*, GAO-11-634 (Washington, D.C.: Sept. 15, 2011).

developing and maintaining an enterprise architecture,[73] and monitoring IT program performance.[74]

In December 2010, OMB issued updated guidance for CIOs, holding them accountable for managing the portfolio of IT projects with the responsibility to terminate or turn around poorly performing projects and retire investments that no longer meet the needs of the organization.[75] As we have previously reported, to carry out these responsibilities effectively, CIOs require sufficient control over IT investments, including control over the IT budget and workforce.[76]

The SSA Commissioner has assigned all of the major CIO functions and responsibilities designated by the Clinger-Cohen Act to the Deputy Commissioner for Systems, thus consolidating major IT management-related functions in a single office. As was the case with the previous CIO, the Deputy Commissioner for Systems reports directly to the Commissioner, which is consistent with the statutory requirement for the CIO to report to the agency head.[77] While the realignment was announced in June 2011, the Commissioner implemented the transfer of responsibilities and staff in several phases. Specifically, the initial realignment transferred the staff responsible for IT strategy, budget, and investment management. In August 2011, the Deputy Commissioner for Systems was assigned the dual responsibility for the CIO and Systems. Also in August, the information security office was transferred from the Office of the CIO to the Office of Systems. Table 2 shows key CIO and Deputy Commissioner for Systems responsibilities prior to and after the realignment.

---

[73]The Clinger-Cohen Act mandate for CIOs to develop and implement agencywide information technology architectures has been implemented under OMB guidance (consistent with GAO best practices) for the development and implementation of enterprise architectures. See GAO-11-634.

[74]40 U.S.C. § 11315(b)(1), (2) and (c)(2).

[75]Office of Management and Budget, *25 Point Implementation Plan to Reform Federal Information Technology Management* (Washington, D.C.: 2010).

[76]GAO-11-634.

[77]44 U.S.C. § 3506(a)(2)(A).

Table 2: Distribution of Key Oversight and Management Responsibilities

Before alignment		After alignment
Office of the CIO	**Office of Systems**	**Office of Systems**
• Oversight of 40% of IT budget • IT investment management (since 2010) • Budget formulation: approve budget and interface with OMB • Workforce planning and allocation of resources to IT projects • Managed cross-cutting portfolio • IT strategic planning and vision • Enterprise architecture: oversight • IT security: policy and oversight • Privacy (shared with Office of General Counsel)	• Management of 60% of IT budget • Systems acquisition, development, and integration • IT investment management (prior to 2010) • IT budget formulation and execution • Enterprise architecture: architecture, engineering, development, and maintenance in support of modernization • IT security: implementation	• Oversight and management of 100% budget formulation and interface with OMB • Systems acquisition, development, and integration • IT investment management process • Workforce planning and allocation of resources to IT projects • IT strategic planning • Manages cross-cutting portfolio • Enterprise architecture: management, vision, strategy, and implementation, architecture, engineering, development, and maintenance • IT security: policy, oversight and implementation • IT operations planning and execution • Privacy (shared with Office of General Counsel)

Source: GAO analysis of SSA data.

As reflected in the table, the realignment merged key responsibilities of the CIO and Deputy Commissioner for Systems into the Office of Systems. Key responsibilities, such as IT investment management and IT strategic planning, were carried out by five offices[78] within the former CIO's organization. Under the realignment, major duties from four of these five offices were transferred to the Office of Systems. As a result, the Deputy Commissioner for Systems has major areas of responsibilities, including 100 percent oversight of the IT investment budget, management of the agency's cross-cutting IT issues, and

---

[78]The former CIO organization's five offices were: the Office of Investment Management, which had IT investment oversight and management responsibilities; the Office of Information Security, which supported IT security policy and oversight; the Office of Innovation and the Office of Vision and Strategy, which supported IT strategic planning and vision; and the Office of Open Government, which fostered the transparency of agency operations and citizen participation, and as such was not part of the key IT investment management and oversight functions.

development and implementation of an enterprise architecture. Specifically, the former CIO Office of Investment Management functions that involved key Clinger-Cohen Act responsibilities, such as capital planning and investment control in selecting, controlling, and evaluating IT investments, were transferred to the Office of Systems, along with the functions of the Office of Information Security.

The major functions of the remaining former CIO offices—the Office of Innovation and the Office of Vision and Strategy—were transferred to the Office of Systems, while some of the staff were reassigned to other SSA components. Specifically, staff members in the Office of Innovation were transferred to the Office of System's Office of Enterprise Support, Architecture, and Engineering.[79] The Office of Vision and Strategy, which was responsible for monitoring agency performance toward strategic goals and supporting the agency's IT planning process, among other things, was divided and transferred, in part to the Office of Systems and in part to various component offices, in June 2011.[80] Finally, the staff and functions from the former CIO Office of Open Government were divided between the Office of Communications and the Office of Operations.

SSA's Realignment Lacked a Plan and an Analysis of Staff Roles and Responsibilities to Support CIO Duties

A management plan based on a thorough analysis of a proposed organizational change should describe the challenges that the agency's management must confront successfully if the goals for the changes are to be accomplished; the plan should also include the strategies for addressing and resolving the challenges, with time frames, resources, performance measures, and accountability structures.[81] An important element of the plan is addressing staffing needs and should include a

---

[79]All of the 18 staff and functions of the Office of Innovation were reassigned to the Office of Systems' Office of Enterprise Support, Architecture and Engineering.

[80]The Office of Vision and Strategy had 26 staff members: 12 staff members from the "strategy" Division of Strategic Services component were reassigned to the Office of Quality Performance; 3 IT Strategy staff members were moved to the Office of Systems, along with functional responsibility for Health IT; other staff members were reassigned to other SSA organization units outside of Office of Systems; and 2 staff members departed the agency.

[81]GAO, *USDA Systems Modernization: Management and Oversight Improvements Are Needed*, GAO-11-586 (Washington, D.C.: July 20, 2011); and GAO-12-226T.

description of the roles and responsibilities that are to be reassigned.[82] Leading practices[83] also stress the importance of major realignments being supported by a comprehensive analysis of the roles and responsibilities needed to support the functions established under the realignment. Included in this plan would be a knowledge and skills inventory to determine skills available in order to decide the proper roles for all employees within the new organization, as well as policies and procedures to manage the staff, and an assessment of personnel requirements. The analysis should include an assessment of core competencies and essential knowledge, skills, and abilities, and identify gaps between current capabilities and those needed to perform established functions. In addition, a detailed analysis of the roles and responsibilities of reassigned employees is needed to support the newly established realignment.

SSA did not develop a plan to address the realignment challenges, including the time frames, staff resources, and how Clinger-Cohen-Act-related duties would be carried out, or perform an analysis of the roles and responsibilities of staff impacted by the organizational change. Instead, according to the Deputy Commissioner for Systems, the realignment was based on cost savings from reducing the number of CIO staff. While the realignment did transfer the number of staff assigned to CIO-related functions by reassigning 33 of the 94 former CIO staff to other Office of Systems components, the overall reduction in staff was minimal.[84] In the absence of an analysis that would define roles and responsibilities, it cannot be determined whether this represents an optimal allocation of resources for carrying out IT oversight and governance.

---

[82]GAO, *Information Technology: FBI Has Largely Staffed Key Modernization Program, but Strategic Approach to Managing Program's Human Capital Is Needed*, GAO-07-19 (Washington, D.C.: Oct. 16, 2006); GAO-12-226T.

[83]GAO-03-669, GAO-03-293SP, GAO-07-844, and GAO-12-226T.

[84]As previously noted, of 144 former CIO staff members, 94 were reassigned to the Office of Systems, 44 were assigned to component offices other than the Office of Systems, and 6 departed the agency.

Guidance for Oversight of IT Portfolios Had Not Been Updated to Reflect the Realignment

While SSA developed IT capital planning and investment control guidance to manage its IT portfolio,[85] the agency had not, as of March 2012, updated this guidance to reflect the recent realignment. This guidance was expected to be updated at the end of 2011. The Deputy Commissioner for Systems and other IT managers stated that the agency was in the process of developing new IT capital planning and investment control guidance. These officials stated that the revised guidance would be reviewed internally beginning at the end of March 2012; however, they could not provide a time line for when the revised guidance would be approved and implemented.

Without updated policy, guidance, and procedures to address SSA's investment review process, it is uncertain whether the newly assigned roles and responsibilities will be effectively carried out. As an example of how the existing guidance does not reflect the realignment, SSA's capital planning and investment control guidance calls for independent CIO reviews of IT investment proposals and requires the CIO and the Deputy Commissioner for Systems to hold discussions to approve certain IT budget decisions. However, given the current structure where the CIO and the Deputy Commissioner for Systems are the same person, these procedures are no longer valid. Additionally, the reassignment of CIO responsibilities has resulted in the elimination of the annual independent CIO review of the IT budget, which is called for by the current guidance.

In discussing this matter, the Deputy Commissioner for Systems stated that the quality of reviews will not change and that the CIO's role of reviewing IT investments will be followed in accordance with capital planning and investment control guidance. However, in light of the multiple changes in various former CIO components and in staff responsibilities, updated oversight guidance is critical to effectively transition to the realignment and maintain effective management of IT investments.

Conclusions

While SSA has undertaken a significant number of projects to modernize its IT environment, major efforts remain to be completed for it to meet its agencywide goals, including strengthening its workforce and

---

[85]SSA, *Fiscal Year 2010 Information Technology Capital Planning and Investment Control Process* (Feb. 12, 2009).

infrastructure to support the growing demands of SSA's services. Specifically, the agency has completed what it identified as key initiatives to help transition from manual, paper-based processes to automated, electronic processes, providing online access to information and services. SSA has also performed a number of enhancements to legacy systems to provide new functionality and, to some extent, reengineered processes and replaced legacy software and applications. While these have yielded benefits in terms of efficiency and customer service, many significant projects are planned or under way for SSA to transition to a modernized environment. Moreover, while SSA has defined performance measures for its ongoing modernization investments, these measures were not always comprehensive, and the agency did not implement our prior recommendation to perform post-implementation reviews of deployed systems, making it uncertain to what extent its efforts are contributing to mission results and goals or whether it is investing in modernization projects in a cost-effective manner.

Compounding the lack of fully comprehensive performance measures to determine modernization progress, SSA has not fully defined a strategic approach to its investment in IT. This approach would include the development and approval of an updated IT strategic plan and a complete enterprise architecture. Without a more strategic and integrated approach to IT, SSA risks making investments that do not support mission needs or position the agency to meet the challenges of increasing workloads.

Finally, SSA has reorganized its IT governance and oversight structure by combining responsibilities of the Office of the CIO and the Office of Systems, which, if implemented appropriately, should allow for effective oversight and management. However, it did so without the benefit of an analysis or plan that would assess challenges and staffing needs arising from the realignment, among other things. Moreover, the agency has yet to define guidance for the oversight of IT investments consistent with its organizational realignment. Clearly defining roles and responsibilities will be a critical component of developing a strategic approach to SSA's ongoing efforts to modernize its IT systems.

Recommendations for Executive Action

To address the challenges facing SSA's IT modernization efforts, we recommend that the Commissioner of Social Security direct the Deputy Commissioner for Systems/Chief Information Officer to take the following four actions:

- Ensure that performance measures in each of OMB's four measurement areas are defined for ongoing IT modernization initiatives and, as appropriate, (1) identify how each investment is to contribute to expected benefits; (2) measure the effectiveness in meeting the goals, requirements, and mission results; and (3) provide a means for measuring projects' progress in meeting modernization goals.

- In updating the IT strategic plan to support the 2013–2016 Agency Strategic Plan, include key elements—such as results-oriented goals, strategies, milestones, performance measures, and an analysis of interdependencies among projects and activities—and use this plan to guide and coordinate IT modernization projects and activities.

- Establish an enterprise architecture plan that includes key components called for by federal guidelines and GAO's enterprise architecture management framework, to effectively guide modernization activities. The plan should include

  - development of a service-oriented architecture road map that guides modernization activities and helps ensure the agency achieves its stated service-oriented architecture goals, such as better business agility and reduced systems development and maintenance costs;

  - development of an enterprise gap analysis that identifies the differences between the current and target environment in all related architecture products;

  - performance targets for the future environment, including interim milestones; and

  - descriptions of relationships among the business processes in terms of information.

- As appropriate, define roles and responsibilities of realigned staff and develop and clearly document updated investment review guidance and procedures to ensure that oversight reviews will be effective in evaluating and controlling investments.

Agency Comments and Our Evaluation

SSA provided written comments on a draft of this report, signed by the Deputy Chief of Staff. The comments are reprinted in appendix II. In its comments, the agency neither agreed nor disagreed with our recommendations; however, it provided responses to each of the recommendations, as well as more general comments on our report's findings.

In its general comments, SSA stated that the title of our draft report suggested that the agency is not successfully modernizing technology and requested that we consider a different title to present a more balanced perspective. We acknowledge that SSA has undertaken many initiatives that have yielded benefits and our intent was not to imply otherwise. However, as emphasized in our report, without a strategic and integrated approach to IT, SSA is at increased risk of making investments that do not support mission needs or position the agency to meet the challenges of increasing workloads. Further, without comprehensive performance measures, the agency is not effectively positioned to know whether it is investing in modernization projects in the most cost-effective manner. As such, these elements are critical to help ensure successful modernization. We have revised the report title to clarify this position.

SSA also stated that our report leaves out modernization efforts and plans, such as its IT security program and modernization efforts associated with its earnings, Supplemental Security Income, and quality assurance processes. Additionally, SSA highlighted the currency of its IT infrastructure and the resulting system performance. In other comments, the agency also questioned our reference to 120 modernization initiatives that it undertook between 2001 and 2011, stating that it did not know how we determined this number of initiatives.

We recognize in our report that SSA has undertaken modernization initiatives and highlighted a broad range of significant examples. During the course of our study, we met with officials representing the agency's core functions, including SSA managers representing five major functional IT areas (Title II, Title XVI, Data Exchange, Enumeration, and Disability). We asked these officials to provide information on what they considered to be the key modernization initiatives completed over the last decade. Our report cites examples of the 120 key modernization initiatives identified by these officials, which include projects in the agency's core functions. As we note, these efforts included enhancing software or providing new functionality for legacy systems, moving from manual to online processes, and developing new software to reengineer processes. We also note in the report that these projects do not represent all of SSA's initiatives over the 11-year period. Nonetheless, based on the agency comments, we added other examples provided by SSA officials, such as its IT operational assurance project. We believe our report provides a valid picture of the agency's modernization efforts and their benefits.

Beyond its general comments, SSA provided various comments on our recommendations. Specifically, regarding our recommendation to ensure that it develop performance measures in each of OMB's four measurement areas and that these measures identify the contribution of each investment to expected benefits; measure their effectiveness in meeting goals, requirements, and mission results; and provide a means for measuring modernization progress, SSA stated that it had been successful in its submissions to OMB in the past and would continue to work with OMB to meet the requirements for developing performance measures in the four required categories, including mission and business results, customer results, processes and activities, and technology. However, as we noted in our report, SSA had not provided measures in all these categories for all of its IT modernization initiatives. Moreover, as we reported, the metrics SSA developed were not comprehensive in that they did not always identify how investments are to contribute to expected benefits, measure effectiveness in meeting mission results, or provide the means for measuring modernization progress. Without such measures, it will be unclear whether or to what extent SSA's efforts are contributing to its goals, and the agency will be limited in its ability to demonstrate to internal and external oversight bodies the success that it believes has resulted from its efforts. Thus, we continue to believe that our recommendation is warranted.

With respect to our recommendation to ensure that its updated IT strategic plan includes key elements such as results-oriented goals, strategies, milestones, performance measures, and an analysis of interdependencies among projects, and to use this plan to guide and coordinate modernization activities, SSA pointed to a draft version of its updated Information Resources Management Plan that it provided to us at the conclusion of our review (and stated that it intends to publish as an approved version at a future date). According to the agency, the updated plan will define the management strategies and process to ensure that IT is aligned with its overall 2013–2016 Agency Strategic Plan, as well as its Agency Performance Plan. However, SSA stated that the purpose of an IRM plan is not to show detailed relationships among projects and activities, and that this analysis and documentation are provided at a project planning level rather than at the enterprise level. We agree that an

IT strategic plan should not include the level of detail that would be provided by individual project documentation—and we did not state in our report that the plan should include this level of detail. However, to be an effective management tool, such a plan should include results-oriented goals, strategies, major milestones, performance measures, and an analysis of interdependencies among projects and activities and clearly link to artifacts providing details on specific projects that support major initiatives. This is to ensure that the agency's IT investment decisions are integrated with its organizational planning, budget, procurement, financial management, human resources management, and program decisions. Further, such a plan provides a needed tool for oversight and accountability and for assessing the agency's progress toward meeting its goals. Thus we believe our recommendation is still warranted.

Regarding our enterprise architecture recommendation, SSA stated that it will comply with recent direction from the Federal Chief Architect to deliver an enterprise architecture roadmap that meets OMB standards, and that it plans to deliver that document in August 2012. The agency added that its approach draws on both the Federal Enterprise Architecture Framework and GAO's architecture framework, while taking into account its specific operational environment and management structure. However, SSA stated that our recommendation regarding a service-oriented architecture roadmap implies an approach that is inconsistent with the agency's approach. Specifically, it stated that it does not intend to comprehensively evaluate its legacy systems to explore opportunities for creating services, but to develop system components as services based on business needs. We agree that SSA should not undertake an assessment of its legacy systems for the sake of exploring opportunities to create services; however, a service-oriented architecture should include a conceptual plan that can be used as a basis for developing detailed project plans and allocating responsibilities to accomplish each of the activities. Such a plan is important since it provides direction and identifies key work that must be performed for SSA to incrementally achieve its vision of reusing services to quickly develop and maintain systems in response to changes in its business environment and reduce the costs of system development and maintenance. Without such a plan, the agency risks not effectively collaborating across organizational components and may not successfully avoid unnecessary duplication and maximize its return on investment.

SSA also took issue with our recommendation to develop an enterprise gap analysis to guide its IT investments. It stated that the identification of gaps in investments arises from its portfolio investment review process and its Application Portfolio Management process. While we agree that investment review processes are key to successful IT management, as we state in our report it is difficult to rely on agency personnel to manage and direct modernization efforts of such a magnitude as SSA's systems without a well-defined enterprise architecture, which should be linked closely to investment control processes. Moreover, SSA's portfolio review and Application Portfolio Management processes focus on addressing gaps for the current fiscal year and do not address enterprise gaps between the current environment and the target environment specified with the 5-year horizon identified by the agency. Further, an enterprise gap analysis would support and inform these processes by providing a strategic, enterprisewide view that may not be available to the officials participating in these efforts. An enterprisewide gap analysis would also help identify common capabilities and unnecessary duplication across organizational components and help determine the relative priority of investments among organizational components and create an enterprisewide transition roadmap for effectively moving to the target environment.

With respect to our recommendation that it develop performance measures and interim milestones for its target architecture, SSA stated that it will continue to improve in this area. Further, the agency discussed its use of "pocket planners" to provide milestones for major proposed investments and help portfolio teams and executives understand the life cycle of each investment and stated these would be included in the EA road map submission to OMB. However, while these documents provide summary information of ongoing individual projects, they do not provide comprehensive and quantitative performance expectations for customer and business process-oriented results, for the investment portfolios in the target environment, or for interim performance milestones. Such information is important to identify performance improvement opportunities and measure the success of each portfolio and its impact on business outcomes.

In addition, with regard to our recommendation to include descriptions of relationships among the business processes in terms of information, SSA disagreed that detailed descriptions of relationships among business processes in terms of information are appropriate for an enterprisewide enterprise architecture plan. Instead, it stated that it describes these relationships for each new development effort. However, as we note in the report, while SSA developed data flow diagrams for specific systems, it has not developed information flows for its current and target environment from a business perspective. This would provide a broad, holistic view of overall business information requirements and how information needs to be shared to support business functions. Such a view would also contribute to improved planning by highlighting the interdependencies in terms of information between each new development effort and other projects and activities. We believe our recommendation would assist SSA in fully addressing OMB A-130 requirements and relevant guidance for developing and using its enterprise architecture.

Finally, regarding our recommendation that it develop and clearly document updated investment review guidance to reflect the CIO realignment and, as appropriate, define roles and responsibilities of realigned staff, SSA stated that it is currently revising its guidance. The agency stated that the guidance will describe the full capital planning and investment control life cycle, including the roles and responsibilities of all participants. These actions, if properly implemented, should help ensure effective oversight of SSA's modernization efforts, and would be consistent with the intent of our recommendation.

SSA also provided technical comments on the draft of this report, which we incorporated as appropriate.

As agreed with your offices, unless you publicly announce the contents of this report earlier, we plan no further distribution until 30 days from the report date. At that time, we will send copies to the Chairman of the Committee on Ways and Means, House of Representatives, the Commissioner of the Social Security Administration, appropriate congressional committees, and other interested parties. In addition, the report will be available at no charge on the GAO website at http://www.gao.gov.

If you or your staff have questions on matters discussed in this report, please contact me at (202) 512-6304 or melvinv@gao.gov. Contact points for our Offices of Congressional Relations and Public Affairs may be found on the last page of this report. GAO staff who made contributions to this report are listed in appendix III.

Sincerely yours,

Valerie C. Melvin
Director
Information Management and Technology Resources Issues

Appendix I: Objectives, Scope, and Methodology

Our objectives were to (1) determine the Social Security Administration's (SSA) progress in modernizing its information technology (IT) systems and capabilities; (2) evaluate the effectiveness of SSA's plans and strategy for modernizing its systems and capabilities; and (3) assess whether the realignment of the agency's Chief Information Officer responsibilities allows for effective oversight and management of the systems modernization efforts.

To determine SSA's progress in modernizing its IT systems and capabilities, we interviewed relevant program officials in five of the agency's major IT functional areas[1] to identify and obtain descriptions of SSA's key completed modernization initiatives from 2001 to 2011. We evaluated project descriptions along with their supporting documentation and compared them against IT modernization activities described in Office of Management and Budget (OMB) exhibit 53 and 300 guidance.[2] We assessed each modernization initiative's purpose, scope, and time frame by interviewing responsible IT managers and evaluating agency documentation to identify the primary type of systems improvements and enhancements and if the initiative redesigned existing processes. We also reviewed SSA's performance metrics for its 17 major IT investments and interviewed responsible IT managers and budget officials to determine how these metrics are applied to individual modernization projects. We compared these measures against guidance from OMB's *Federal Enterprise Architecture*, the Government Performance and Results Act, the Paperwork Reduction Act, and the Clinger-Cohen Act. In addition, we reviewed agency IT project plans, milestones, goals, budgets, briefings, IT investment review board minutes, and post-release reviews to determine its modernization efforts and progress.

In addressing the second objective, we evaluated the agency's IT plans and strategies for modernizing its systems against guidance in OMB's

---

[1]The five major IT functional areas were: Title II: Administering disability, old age, and survivor benefits; Title XVI: Administering Supplemental Security Income; Data Exchange: sending and receiving electronic information with third parties; Enumeration: Allocation and verification of Social Security numbers; and Disability: Determination, control, and tracking of disability claims.

[2]The exhibit 300—the Capital Asset Plan and Business Case—is to justify each request for a major IT investment. In addition each federal agency reports its IT investment portfolio annually to OMB via an exhibit 53. The exhibit 53 provides budget estimates for all IT investments and identifies those that are major investment and nonmajor investments.

Circular A-130, Management of Federal Information Resources. We
assessed SSA's planning documentation and interviewed the Deputy
Commissioner for Systems and Office of Systems managers on the
agency's plans and time frames to update its IT strategic plan.
Additionally, we evaluated the agency's enterprise architecture
documentation against OMB's *Federal Enterprise Architecture* guidance
and our enterprise architecture framework[3] to determine the effectiveness
of its enterprise architecture in describing and supporting its systems and
capabilities modernization efforts. We also discussed with SSA's
technology leadership the agency's approach to modernization and its
challenges in developing a modern and efficient IT environment in the
future.

In order to address the third objective, we assessed SSA's plans and
analyses of the reassignment of Office of the Chief Information Officer
duties and functions to determine if the realignment allowed for effective
IT oversight and management activities. We also reviewed
documentation, such as updated agency policy, memos, and IT review
board minutes and compared this information to best practices to assess
the agency's plans and analyses of the realignment. Additionally, we
interviewed the Chief Information Officer and other IT executives about
their roles and responsibilities under the new IT realignment.

To assess the reliability of the data that we used to support the findings in
this report, we reviewed relevant program documentation to substantiate
evidence obtained through interviews with agency officials. We
determined that the data used in this report are sufficiently reliable. We
have also made appropriate attribution indicating the sources of the data.

We conducted this performance audit from May 2011 to April 2012 in
accordance with generally accepted government auditing standards.
Those standards require that we plan and perform the audit to obtain
sufficient, appropriate evidence to provide a reasonable basis for our
findings and conclusions based on our audit objectives. We believe that
the evidence obtained provides a reasonable basis for our findings and
conclusions based on our audit objectives.

---

[3]GAO-10-846G.

SOCIAL SECURITY
Office of the Commissioner

April 13, 2012

Ms. Valerie C. Melvin
Director, Information Management and Technology Resources Issues
United States Government Accountability Office
441 G. Street, NW
Washington, D.C. 20548

Dear Ms. Melvin:

Thank you for the opportunity to review the draft report, "SOCIAL SECURITY
ADMINISTRATION: Improved Planning and Performance Measures Are Needed to
Successfully Modernize Technology" (GAO-12-495). Our response is enclosed.

If you have any questions, please contact me at (410) 965-0520. Your staff may contact
John Biles, Acting Director, Audit Liaison Staff, at (410) 965-3758.

Sincerely,

Dean S. Landis
Deputy Chief of Staff

Enclosure

SOCIAL SECURITY ADMINISTRATION   BALTIMORE, MD 21235-0001

**COMMENTS ON THE GOVERNMENT ACCOUNTABILITY OFFICE (GAO) DRAFT
REPORT, "SOCIAL SECURITY ADMINISTRATION: IMPROVED PLANNING AND
PERFORMANCE MEASURES ARE NEEDED TO SUCCESSFULLY MODERNIZE
TECHNOLOGY" (GAO-12-495)**

GENERAL COMMENTS

This was an extremely broad audit, and we appreciate the challenges the GAO review team faced
in attempting to understand our large and complex business and information technology (IT)
environment. During the 10-month period of this audit, we participated in over 40 meetings with
GAO and provided approximately 125 detailed responses to requests for information. Please see
our technical comments below regarding clarifications and corrections.

As a general matter, we object to the title of this report. It implies we are not successfully
modernizing technology when extensive facts prove otherwise. We request that you consider a
more balanced title that is more consistent with your report, such as "Technology Modernization
Would Benefit from Improved Planning and Performance Measures."

Your draft report references a number of our modernization efforts and plans, but it leaves others
out. In particular, we note the absence of our e-service applications, our well regarded IT
security program, and IT modernization efforts associated with earnings, Supplemental Security
Income, and quality assurance processes. These are all core functions of the agency. We are
also proud of the overall technical currency of our IT operations and telecommunications
infrastructure, and the resulting 99.9 percent effective systems performance in the agency.

RESPONSE TO RECOMMENDATIONS

Recommendation 1

Ensure that performance measures in each of OMB's four measurement areas are defined for
ongoing IT modernization initiatives and, as appropriate, that measures: (1) identify how each
investment is to contribute to expected benefits; (2) the effectiveness in meeting the goals,
requirements, and mission results; (3) provide a means for measuring projects' progress in
meeting modernization goals.

Response

This recommendation refers to the Office of Management and Budget's (OMB) requirements for
the Exhibit 300, IT Capital Asset Summary and Performance Measurement Report. We have
been successful in our submissions to OMB in the past, and we will continue to work with OMB
to meet every requirement of its guidance, including meaningful and objectively measureable
performance measures for each category required within Exhibit 300's mission and business
results, customer results, processes and activities, and technology.

Recommendation 2

In updating the IT strategic plan to support the 2013-2016 Agency Strategic Plan, include key elements, such as results-oriented foals, strategies, milestones, performance measures, and an analysis of interdependencies among projects and activities, and use this plan to guide and coordinate IT modernization projects and activities.

Response

Our updated Information Resource Management (IRM) Strategic Plan is in final clearance and we expect to publish it within the next month. Our IRM plan defines the management strategy and processes that ensure IT is aligned with the initiatives defined in our 2013 – 2016 Agency Strategic Plan (ASP), and that our IT supports our Agency Performance Plan (APP). The IRM plan includes project level milestones that must occur to ensure fulfillment of the ASP and supporting APP performance objectives.

However, it is not the purpose of the IRM plan to show the detailed interrelationships among projects and activities. We provide that analysis and documentation at a project planning level. We develop our IRM plan at the enterprise level. While the IRM plan provides an enterprise-level view of our projects and activities, we support the coordination of those projects and activities with planning documents at the appropriate level of the organization. To guide this management activity, we have fully developed life cycle guidance that supports all development activities, not just those associated with modernization initiatives.

Recommendation 3

Establish an enterprise architecture plan that includes key components called for by federal guidelines and the GAO enterprise architecture management framework, to effectively guide modernization activities. The plan should include,

- development of a service-oriented architecture road map that guides modernization activities and helps ensure the agency achieves its stated service-oriented architecture goals, such as better business agility and reduced systems development and maintenance costs;
- development of an enterprise gap analysis that identifies the difference between the current and target environment in all related architecture products;
- performance targets for the future environment, including interim milestones; and
- descriptions of relationships among the business processes in terms of information.

Response

We will comply with recent direction from the Federal Chief Architect to deliver an Enterprise Architecture (EA) roadmap that meets OMB standards. The current delivery date for that documentation is August 2012. OMB has historically accepted our EA submissions without

2

objection or correction, and we expect that this next deliverable will also meet with OMB's approval. We will comply with OMB's guidelines for content and scope of the EA roadmap. We will undertake this activity for all components of our IT environment, not only our modernization activities.

We also respect GAO's architecture framework, and we use it as guidance as we meet OMB's requirements. GAO Executive Guide, "*ORGANIZATIONAL TRANSFORMATION: A Framework Assessing and Improving Enterprise Architecture Management (Version 2.0)*" GAO-10-846G, states in the preface:

> *Managed properly, an EA can help simplify, streamline, and clarify the interdependencies and relationships among an organization's diverse mission and mission-support operations and information needs, including its associated IT environment. When employed in concert with other institutional management disciplines, such as strategic planning, portfolio-based capital planning and investment control, and human capital management, an EA can greatly increase the chances of configuring an organization to promote agility and responsiveness, optimize mission performance and strategic outcomes, and address new federal initiatives like promoting open and participatory government and leveraging cloud computing.*

Our institutional IT management disciplines include strategic planning, Strategic Information Technology Assessment and Review (SITAR), portfolio management, Application Portfolio Management (APM), and Capital Planning and Investment Control (CPIC) processes. Our EA processes exist in this IT management ecosystem. Using the tools in our environment, we have successfully addressed mission outcomes, new Federal initiatives, legislative mandates, and court-ordered actions. On page 2 of the GAO Executive Guide, the preface states:

> *In summary, version 2.0 builds on the prior version by introducing considerably more scope and content to accommodate the evolving and complex nature of EA as one of many enterprise management disciplines and the practical realities surrounding actual EA development and use. As such, this version of the framework provides a more current and pragmatic construct for viewing EA development and use. In this regard, it provides a flexible benchmark against which to plan for and measure EA program management maturity that permits thoughtful and reasonable discretion to be applied in using it. Restated, the framework is not intended to be a rigidly applied 'one size fits all' checklist, but rather a flexible frame of reference that should be applied in a manner that makes sense for each organization's unique facts and circumstances. Moreover, the framework is not intended to be viewed as the sole bench marking tool for informing and understanding an organization's journey toward EA maturity.*

With OMB's Federal Enterprise Architecture Framework defining our EA products and GAO's architecture framework providing additional advice, we developed an approach that takes into account our specific operational and management context. Using the flexibility accorded by the GAO framework, we developed an Enterprise Architecture strategy that integrates smoothly into

3

our management ecosystem and forms a coherent management framework in concert with our other oversight and control systems.

The recommendation regarding a Service-Oriented Architecture (SOA) road-map implies an approach to developing services that is inconsistent with our approach, which we based on our requirements and best practices. We do not intend to evaluate our legacy systems simply to explore opportunities to create services. Rather, as we begin our planning for developing new functionality or modernization, we look for opportunities to develop system components as services. We do not develop services for the sake of SOA. We invest to obtain business outcomes, and we use those investments to build out our SOA environment. We continue to better define the processes through which we identify and leverage opportunities to develop service components, but we do not intend to develop an enterprise-wide road map to guide our efforts.

You recommend that we develop an enterprise gap analysis to guide our IT investments. Rather than evaluating the entire enterprise from a central perspective all at once, we provide guidance to the organizational component that has responsibility for the business process to assess their current state, its objectives, and to identify gaps. This analysis becomes the basis for the decision of what IT projects to bring to SITAR through the portfolio process. The APM process accomplishes the same identification of investment opportunities as enterprise gap analysis where we evaluate existing applications on several factors to determine whether they are appropriate candidates for renovation or renewal. Although this report implies that the dominant planning process should be the EA, we rely on an IT investment process that includes explicit involvement of the business units through the SITAR process, and is a superior approach given our management and technology environment.

We are continually evolving and improving our IT investment and management processes. We have already noted your recommendation regarding performance measures, and we will continue to improve in that area. The SITAR process requires the consistent use of pocket planners by the portfolio teams. These planners provide milestones for major proposed investments, which help the portfolio teams and our executives understand the intended life cycle of each investment. We also require a multi-year strategic business plan for each portfolio. We will include these business plans in the roadmap submission to OMB in August 2012.

Descriptions of relationships among our business process exist at many levels. We carefully and explicitly describe these relationships as we undertake every new development effort. The descriptions exist in documentation for security certification as well. While a high-level informational description might be appropriate for an enterprise-wide EA plan, we do not agree that detailed descriptions are appropriate for such a plan. As we have already stated, we intend to fully comply with OMB requirements for EA planning.

4

Recommendation 4

As appropriate, define roles and responsibilities of realigned staff and develop and clearly document updated investment review guidance and procedures to ensure that oversight reviews will be effective in evaluating and controlling investments.

Response

We are currently revising our CPIC guide, which will describe the full CPIC life cycle, including the roles and responsibilities of all participants. Specifically, Section 4, "*Agency Roles and Responsibilities*" defines, in part, current Office of Systems/Chief Information Officer functions in the selection, control and evaluation phases of IT investments. Section 3 of the guide details processes and procedures for each investment phase (select, control, and evaluate), including review and oversight functions.

5

Appendix III: GAO Contact and Staff Acknowledgments

GAO Contact	Valerie C. Melvin at (202) 512-6304 or melvinv@gao.gov
Staff Acknowledgments	In addition to the contact named above, Christie Motley (Assistant Director), Michael Alexander, Neil Doherty, Rebecca Eyler, Nancy Glover, David Hong, Alina J. Johnson, Anh Le, John C. Martin, Lee McCracken, Madhav Panwar, and Scott Pettis made key contributions to this report.

www.ingramcontent.com/pod-product-compliance
Lightning Source LLC
Chambersburg PA
CBHW081140290526
45795CB00006B/2319